ANiMATiNG your CAREER

ANiMATiNG your CAREER

STEVE HiCKNER

BRIGANTINE MEDIA

Animating Your Career

Illustrations by Steve Hickner

Cover and Book Design by Jacob L. Grant

ISBN 978-1-9384062-8-7

Brigantine Media
211 North Avenue, St. Johnsbury, Vermont 05819
Phone: 802-751-8802
Email: neil@brigantinemedia.com
Website: www.brigantinemedia.com

For Laura and Cindy—
The women who defined the first two Acts of my life.

CONTENTS

CONTENTS

FOREWORD

If you're like me, you grew up watching great animation, and never thought twice about how it was done, until one day it dawned on you that there were people who actually got paid to make animated films! Seriously! That was a day that changed my life. My curiosity about the art of animation led to a lot of hard work, great friendships, and thrilling opportunities in one of the greatest industries on Earth: animation.

When I started over thirty years ago, animation was an industry that had fallen asleep. Disney was making a new animated feature every three or four years. There was no Pixar, DreamWorks, Illumination, or Blue Sky, and the animation business felt like a children's theater compared to the glamorous stars, huge box office, and dazzling effects of the mainstream film business. Today, all that has changed! Animation is a booming, dazzling, and profitable business full of opportunity, and a business that needs people to create the modern miracles that are today's animated features.

From the outside, animation looks like a complicated, daunting group of studios behind mysterious guarded gates which you, as a beginner, may never dream of entering. Now there's someone to help show you the way.

Steve Hickner has written a book that I wish I had owned when I was a young artist. He's laid out all the opportunities and pitfalls of the business in a fun-to-read book that can be the start of an amazing adventure making films, games, television shows, and special effects films that entertain people around the world. Steve is a pro's pro and one of the few people who has done nearly everyone's job in this complex world, including directing some of the brightest and best animated features out there.

Now he hands you a great gift in the pages of this book, and a road map in the form of his vast personal experiences and advice. Eat it up, work hard, have fun, be prepared, and add just a little luck, and you'll be able to enjoy an incredible life in the animation world.

Good luck!

Don Hahn

Don Hahn

PREFACE

I can recall with vivid clarity the moment I first saw the sign, "Los Angeles, 500 miles." For me, the idea of working in the movies was not only a dream—it was a dare. Would I have what it took to make it in Hollywood? Taking on that challenge has led me on an adventure that has lasted three decades and given me more satisfaction than I could have imagined.

Wow! When I realize I have managed to stick around making cartoons for thirty years while working with some of the most wonderful people imaginable, I have to pinch myself. Even though I moved to Los Angeles without any show business connections, I do not consider myself to be a "self-made man." The fact is, I have been the beneficiary of the people who have helped, molded, and mentored me. But as I look back, I realize I have learned rules, tips, and bits of advice that might be beneficial to others. After all, I didn't come from a well-connected family or possess extraordinary abilities, and if I could set my sights on a dream and reach it, you can too.

I have tried to create a book that will help you take advantage of the wisdom that has been passed down to me. Sadly, too many of my betters are gone, and these pages will be my chance to keep their thoughts alive. The first part of this book will focus on how to go about getting the job you want, and what you can do to build career longevity once you land that job. The most competitive fields are also the ones with the highest turnover rates. So if you are not careful, you can fall out of favor and be back on the outside looking in once again. In the second part of the book, I will show you how to become an indispensable team leader. The longer you stay in a profession, the more likely it will be that you will gain supervisory responsibilities. It can be frightening when you realize that your worth to the company is no longer dependent on your individual productivity but rather on the success of your team. I will offer you some guidance to facilitate this transition.

These rules work in other fields of endeavor. Although the motion picture industry might have a higher profile than some businesses, the traits that make someone successful in the world of entertainment are the same ones that allow a person to be successful in any walk of life. Good work habits can help anyone become better at what he/she does.

I've written this book for every person who dreams of a creative career. I'm going to give you lots of suggestions and I hope some of it will be helpful in your personal journey. All of this advice comes from my heart. If you have a burning desire to advance in a creative career, then I think this book will help you. Because when you follow your passion … well, to quote the title of a Christmas perennial, "It's a Wonderful Life."

INTRODUCTION

"Study the past if you would define the future."
—Confucius

Here is a tip that will be of immense help if you want to succeed: Learn the history of your business.

Not long ago, I gave a talk about my career in animation to a dozen students from colleges and universities all over the United States. These were big name schools with distinctive creative programs, and the young people were selected from a huge pool of candidates. Every student was a film, communications, or media arts major. I had invited the students to meet with me because I was interested in learning about their film programs, and I had hoped that we could enjoy a lively discussion about movies. We spoke for about ninety minutes, and when the group departed, I stayed behind in a state of shock.

In that hour and a half conversation, not one student had seen any of the films that I mentioned.

Now, let me confess that I have an eclectic taste in movies, and I see a fair amount of independent, documentary, and foreign films. Therefore, some of the movies that I referenced might not be familiar, but I also mentioned *The Godfather, Chinatown,* and *Citizen Kane.* I would excuse the fact that no one had seen any of these titles if I were talking to economics majors, but these were film students!

I work in a profession where your homework is an excuse to watch some of the greatest films of all time. How difficult is that assignment? If you want to make movies, you must also be a consumer of movies.

This lack of curiosity about the history of cinema is not confined to film students. Kevin Lima, a director whose credits include the Disney films *Enchanted* and *Tarzan,* told me that in one of his story meetings, he referenced Robert Zemeckis's *Romancing the Stone.* To his amazement, no one in the room had seen the film. These were film professionals, and yet they had not seen an important movie in their field.

When I am speaking to a group of future filmmakers who have not seen any movies, I wonder if they are following the right path.

WHEN YOU'RE LOOKING FOR A JOB, GIVE THEM WHAT THEY'RE LOOKING FOR

Have you ever tried to sell something to someone who doesn't need it? You probably met with rejection because you didn't do your homework to find the people who were buying what you were selling. The same rule is true when you are hunting for that great job.

I once spoke with two college students from different parts of the country. The first student called to ask about career advice, and he was hoping that I would supply him with a list of animation companies where he could apply, as well as their contact information. I explained to him that I could not possibly give him the names of prospective companies because I had no idea what his interests were. Did he prefer the cartoony world of TV animation, or the naturalistic genre of first person computer games? Were there any individuals that inspired his work? Were there people whom he admired? He only had vague replies to my answers and I soon realized that he had not done any research into the field he was about to enter. He didn't know any of the players in animation, nor was he familiar with the types of animation that the different studios produced.

If I were an employer looking to hire an artist, he would have blown the interview.

Only a couple of days prior to my conversation with this student, I met with another college student and my impression was just the opposite. As she began to question me, it was clear that she had done extensive research into my background. Not only had she done her homework on me, but she had also spoken to some of my peers and had stories from them about projects that I had worked on.

If I were an employer looking to hire an artist, she would start Monday.

The reason the well-prepared student would be such a clear-cut hire is because she is giving the employer what he/she is looking for: an employee already familiar with the company's history and product. She would be selling exactly what the company is buying. In contrast, the college student that I spoke to on the phone came across as lazy. He wanted me to do all his homework by supplying him with the names and backgrounds of companies and people who might hire him. The fact is, I would never recommend a person who knows so little about the field he is entering. Here's an incredibly obvious tip, but one that seems to be unknown to a lot of people trying to enter the market: *If you want to know what people will buy, look at what they have already bought.*

In 1990, Walt Disney animation released an animated short to accompany their main feature, *The Rescuers Down Under*. The short was a retelling of Mark Twain's classic story, *The Prince and the*

Pauper, and included Mickey Mouse playing both of the title roles. At the time, Jeffrey Katzenberg was in charge of the animation department at Disney, and his decision to greenlight the project did not surprise me. Why? Because seven years earlier, while in charge of the motion picture division at Paramount Pictures, Katzenberg had produced *Trading Places*—an updated version of *The Prince and the Pauper* starring Eddie Murphy and Dan Ackroyd. The fact is, Jeffrey Katzenberg likes the story of *The Prince and the Pauper*. If you had a gritty movie script about gangsters in New York City, wouldn't you pitch the project to Martin Scorsese? I would. And so did the people who had the story for *Revenge of the Green Dragons*. I guess they figured that the guy who made *Mean Streets*, *Taxi Driver*, *Gangs of New York*, *Raging Bull*, and *Goodfellas* might like a story with an edge set in New York.

Do not begin your job search until you've done your due diligence. Take inventory of what interests you, and also learn as much as you can about the people and companies who produce the work and products you enjoy. In today's web-enhanced world, there is no excuse for stepping into the job hunting arena ill-prepared—yet my experience is that most people do.

PART I

MAKiNG your DREAM HAPPEN

1

THE LEAPING FROG AND THE PATIENT SNAKE

*"There is no man living who isn't capable of doing
more than he thinks he can do."*
—Henry Ford

"Three frogs are sitting on a log, and two decide to jump. How many are left?"

The answer is "three"—because deciding to jump and actually jumping are not the same. Potential is not sufficient to achieve a result. All of us have known talented people who have never achieved the success they should have achieved. Like the frogs, these people fail to "jump" and convert their potential into success. Life is not fair. All of us have different abilities. Some people are born taller, smarter, prettier, more handsome, or more talented than we are. Many of these traits are embedded into our DNA and we cannot change them. If you are one of the lucky ones to be blessed with such gifts, congratulations—you have a head start in life. But even if you did not inherit terrific assets, great opportunities are still possible. Life may not be fair, but it does allow room for negotiating. While we are all given a set of tools at the start, such as intelligence and talent, the amount to which we develop these abilities is up to us.

And that is our big escape clause.

When I was growing up, I adored the work of Charles M. Schulz for his comic strip, "Peanuts." He was one of my heroes, and I did my best to absorb as much of his drawing techniques as possible. There were many individual strips that I enjoyed, but I especially recall one drawing of Linus Van Pelt, the brilliant philosopher of the strip. Because of his intelligence, he carried the weight of great expectations. As he once famously observed, "There's no heavier burden than a great potential." Linus's words are bitingly true; having great potential is nothing but a promissory note.

Steven Spielberg possesses an extraordinary talent for making movies, but before he achieved success, he was just another young wannabe filmmaker. Then one day he made the "jump" and snuck onto the Universal Studios lot. He hung around the movie sets, watching TV shows like *Wagon Train* being filmed and becoming a presence in the editing rooms. Eventually, he became such a fixture at the studio, the guards thought that he belonged there, and he managed to appropriate an empty office. He was able to get an audience for his short film, *Amblin*, and the rest became history.

When I begin a job, it is the frog in me that gets me to jump into the fray, but it's the snake in me that keeps me going, bit by bit. What do I mean by "the snake in me?" Let me explain...

Snakes have been on earth since the days of the dino-saurs, and for good reason. They are adaptable. Despite their ubiquity, snakes are the recipients of a great deal of bad press. For instance, most people think that a boa constrictor kills its

prey by squeezing it to death. In actuality, a boa constrictor kills its prey in a less theatrical way. The snake grabs its lunch-to-be within its coils, and patiently waits for the animal to inhale. Each time the animal takes a breath, the snake tightens its coils until the prey is unable to breathe. The prey simply dies from suffocation. The boa constrictor may not be as fast as a cheetah or as cagey as a wolf, but this snake is every bit as successful at securing its dinner. The boa constrictor is the model of accomplishment through persistence.

Perhaps the thought of being compared to a serpent is not appealing to you, but the boa constrictor's success is proof that you can achieve the same result as others who are swifter or smarter. Discipline yourself for incremental gain. You can arrive at the same place as your peers by sticking to a job and being persistent. Before you begin a task, imagine the pleasure of the result and use this future reward for the impetus to begin and the conviction to continue through adversity.

I have used self-discipline to my advantage during my career. When others around me arrive late, pack up early, relax on self-improvement, let their skills slide, or fail to study the horizon for how the business will be changing, I gain ground on them. I take pride in being a reliable and dedicated animation professional. There is no training or waiting period necessary to develop self-determination. You can start today. All you have to do is to decide you want to reach a certain goal—and make the commitment to keep working at it until you get there. You do not have to achieve your goal in one burst. Focus your attention on improving your abilities or situation a little bit at a time, and eventually you will arrive at your destination.

ATTITUDE IS ALL

When I was living in London and working for Steven Spielberg, the studio was so new that we had to hire almost 200 employees. During our search for talent, I realized that I valued a particular character trait even more than technical proficiency. The magical component that is so important that it supersedes the benefits of a high IQ or brilliant talent is …

Attitude.

In addition to self-control, self-determination, and persistence, attitude is another one of those jewels that we possess that is independent of our DNA. While we may not be able to make ourselves smarter on a daily basis, we can influence our job outlook and mood. Deciding to bring a great attitude into each work situation is perhaps the single most important decision you can make. There is no simpler way to improve your odds of career longevity than by being known as a person who brings enthusiasm to the office. Kelly Asbury, the director of *Shrek 2*, *Gnomeo and Juliet,* and *Spirit: Stallion of the Cimarron*, has a great reputation for being fun to work with. And guess what? He is always in demand. No sound engineer has to duck a flying coffee mug on a Kelly Asbury film—although I have heard tales of such insanity taking place on other people's movie sets.

As a producer, I hired dozens of artists and production crewmembers, and I always chose the person with the best attitude if the decision was a close one. I can teach someone the technical requirements of a job, but I cannot teach someone to have a good attitude. I have witnessed both excellent and poor attitudes in the work environment and in college classrooms, and I know that being around a worker or student who is negative impacts the dynamic for the entire group. When the situation calls for creative collaboration, having a healthy environment is essential and the candidate who is eager to help is the kind of person that I want beside me in the foxholes.

I have worked alongside Jeffrey Katzenberg for over half of my career and I can attest to the fact that you are unlikely to find anyone with a more positive attitude. Katzenberg has been one of the most successful studio executives over the past few decades and he considers enthusiasm such an important attribute for a career aspirant that he places it on par with the pursuit of excellence. In a May 2008 speech to graduates of the Ringling College School of Arts he said, "Whatever you do, do it really, really well and with lots of enthusiasm ...and if you're the one putting maximum energy into whatever you're doing, not only will you move ahead on your path more quickly, but you will be more engaged and have more fun along the way. And I promise—you will stand out." Not everyone, however, is naturally gregarious or outgoing. In such circumstances, there is another trick to employ:

ACT THE PART, AND YOU'LL BECOME THE PART

Cary Grant is considered the epitome of the suave, sophisticated gentleman, but according to Grant, his persona was something that he developed over time. He once said, "I don't know that I've any style at all. I just patterned myself on a combination of Jack Buchanan, Noel Coward, and Rex Harrison. I pretended to be somebody I wanted to be and I finally became that person. Or he became me. Or we met at some point. It's a relationship." (Richard Schickel, "The Acrobat of the Drawing Room," *Time,* January 26, 2007)

When I arrived in London to work as an associate producer on *An American Tail II: Fievel Goes West*, I was worried that I would not be gregarious enough to serve as a leader for the large crew. In

 order to do the best job, I decided that I would play the part and force myself to be much more outgoing than I actually was.

Several months into

the production, I was working alongside one of the department supervisors when she remarked that she was impressed by how energetic and enthusiastic I always seemed to be. I confided in her that my whole demeanor was an act—I was quite shy and I was just pretending to be extroverted. She looked at me incredulously and replied, "No, you're not. I'm here with you for ten hours a day, and you are always enthusiastic. Nobody could act for that long. That's the way you are." As I listened to her words, I realized that she was right. I was outgoing. I had acted the part for so long that I had become what I was pretending to be. Just as Cary Grant had said, at some point the acting gave way to actual behavior.

Anyone can do it. The only prerequisite is that you must possess the desire to change. Once you start practicing having a great attitude, each successive day will become easier. Before you know it, you will be the person that everyone points to as the one they want on their team.

2

NEVER TURN DOWN a COMBat Mission

"To eat an egg, you must break the shell."
—Jamaican Proverb

Chalmers Goodlin is not a name most people will recognize. He loved airplanes and by the time he was fifteen, he was taking flying lessons. His love affair with flight blossomed and after a stint with the Royal Canadian Air Force, he was hired by Bell Aircraft Corporation as a test pilot. And for a test pilot at Bell Aircraft (under a contract from the Air Force), the prize was the X-1— because that was the plane built to break the sound barrier.

Back in 1947, there were plenty of engineers and pilots who believed that supersonic flight was a threshold that could not be passed. Still, the Air Force pressed on, and Chalmers "Slick" Goodlin was chosen as the pilot to guide the X-1 into history as the first plane to break the sound barrier. But Chalmers Goodlin never made that historic flight. He was not the first to take the X-1 supersonic, and there are no plaques to commemorate his flight or photos for the archives. You see, the X-1 was so experimental as a plane, and the concept of supersonic flight so precarious, that Goodlin wanted a bonus for the job—a $150,000 bonus.

The Air Force refused this request and instead asked another pilot to fly the X-1. That pilot said "Yes," and on the 14th of October in 1947, earning only his monthly captain's pay of $283, Chuck Yeager stepped into the history books as the first person to break the sound barrier. Books have been written about Captain Charles E. Yeager. In fact, Sam Shepard immortalized him in the film, *The Right Stuff.* All of the accolades and fame Chuck Yeager has received are because he took one simple axiom to heart:

"Never turn down a combat mission. You never know where it will lead."

History is full of people and organizations that have turned down opportunities that later became massive successes elsewhere. On New Year's Day in 1962, two musical groups auditioned for Decca Records. After much deliberation, the label chose Brian Poole and the Tremeloes with the reasoning, "guitar groups are on the way out." Thus Dick Rowe became known as "the guy who turned down the Beatles." Several publishing houses rejected the story of a boy wizard written by an unknown writer before Bloomsbury finally agreed to publish the first of what would become seven *Harry Potter* books. Warner Brothers declined the rights to release *Slumdog Millionaire*, allowing Fox Searchlight to step in and snag the 2009 Best Picture Oscar winner and worldwide smash. And Warner Brothers passed on the property not after reading a script, but after seeing the film! Successful companies do not make a habit of missing good opportunities, but when they do, they are often large enough to recover from the misstep. You do not have the same resources as a company, and so you need to capitalize on breaks whenever they are presented. Unlike a big recording label, a huge movie studio, or a publishing giant, a missed opportunity for you might spell the difference between a bright career and a "Whatever Became of..." trivia question.

The maxim of "Never turn down a combat mission" and using Chuck Yeager's supersonic flight as an example belongs to a terrific cartoonist named Warren Greenwood. Warren and I shared a room together when we were working as storyboard artists on *He-Man and the Masters of the Universe*. As storyboard artists, our role was to translate the written words of the script into pictures. The final result was similar to a comic book and allowed the other departments to work from our visualizations of the story.

When *He-Man and the Masters of the Universe* got the green light for sixty-five episodes, it was a landmark. Orders for new television shows routinely were for thirteen episodes and the *He-Man* crew would need to produce five times the usual amount. With the increased load, the Filmation executives felt they needed some help for their storyboard supervisor, Bob Arkwright. Arkwright considered his storyboard staff and somehow decided that I would be the best candidate for his new assistant storyboard supervisor. When Arkwright made me the offer, I had never considered being a manager of any kind. All I wanted to do was draw and make films, and I felt a managerial role would lead me away from that goal. Into that mix of opportunity and apprehension entered Warren Greenwood.

Now, if you were going to call central casting and ask them to send over the most anti-establishment artistic type that they could find, Warren Greenwood would be the guy who would show up. Greenwood was a voracious reader who, quite fortuitously, was reading Tom Wolfe's *The Right Stuff*. When I came back from Arkwright's office mulling over the offer, I shared my news with him. Instead of trying to dissuade me from taking the job, Greenwood urged me to accept. And by way of emphasis, he spoke the words that I have never forgotten: "You know what Chuck Yeager would say? *Never turn down a combat mission.*"

The more Greenwood spoke, the more I realized that I did not want to become another footnote to history. To my own surprise, I took the job and was grateful for the chance to pick up some valuable managing skills. After that first positive experience, I decided that I would always say "Yes!" to opportunity.

The cumulative result of remaining receptive to new challenges has opened new career paths for me. For instance, during the mid-eighties, Disney Studios was undergoing an enormous transformation in their animation department. Michael Eisner and Jeffrey Katzenberg had left Paramount and come to Disney with the goal of rejuvenating the moribund family entertainment company. Among the flotsam and jetsam of the previous regime was an animated short starring Goofy. By the time the Goofy film was finished, the climate at the studio had changed and the project was cast aside. Ed Hansen, a longtime Disney executive, still believed there was value in a project starring one of the Studio's mainstay characters, and brought together a team of four artists to revitalize the short. Since most of the money for the project had already been spent, and there was no real market for a twenty-plus minute short film, the project was in the priorities basement.

When Ed first broached the idea of resurrecting the project, there were many Disney artists who had no desire to toil away on a project that had an iffy future. At the time, I was just one in a huge department of assistant animators, so I jumped at the chance to work on the project when the offer came. There were four of us on the re-imagining team: Matt O'Callaghan, Joe Lanzisero, Barry Temple, and me. As we began to shore up the story, I realized that there was a huge administrative void. Because I was the only member of the team who enjoyed the planning and managing part of the process, I became the de facto production manager. I had never managed a production before and, although some studio personnel were wary of giving me the chance, Ed Hansen backed me and I made it through the process. I would love to report that the project was a huge success, but I would be rewriting history. In fact, the short film became the cornerstone of a forgettable NBC-TV special that languished at the bottom of that week's ratings. Most people would say that the time spent on the project was a waste of time—but they would be wrong.

Despite the show's dubious merit, my career gained an unexpected boost. By taking on an unpopular project, I was able to work as a production manager—an opportunity that never would have presented itself if I had stayed on the main Disney feature films. Up to that point, I had only worked as an artist in the animation business, and now I had some experience working on the production side as well. When shortly thereafter, Richard Dreyfuss brought an idea to the studio for a TV special saluting the United States Constitution, I was paired with Disney veteran Dave Michener to create the animated segments. This project was also not considered high priority, as most of the top studio animators were working on the feature film, *Oliver and Company*.

With my new assignment on the Constitution special, I was now associated with not one, but two projects that most of the other artists avoided. Furthermore, the two projects possessed the deadly trinity of production woes: a short schedule, a low budget, and few resources. Even though every sign pointed to avoid these projects at all costs, I happily took the jobs because I needed the experience. While I was working on those two hand-me-down projects at Disney, I was optimistic that they would improve me in some unknown fashion. What I could never have foreseen was that those television jobs that no one wanted would steer me into the path of one of the most important experiences of my career: working on the 1988 landmark film, *Who Framed Roger Rabbit?*

THE JOB/CAREER BUTTERFLY EFFECT

As true as the axiom of "Never turn down a combat mission" may be, the wisdom only represents half of the critical information. The second part of that Chuck Yeager rule should read: *"Because you never know where it will lead."* The maxim is, in effect, a career-path version of the "butterfly effect." Most of us have heard variations of the butterfly effect—the theory that the world is so interconnected that a butterfly flapping its wings in the Amazon will have a tremendous impact on an apparently unconnected event such as coffee prices in Canada. I believe the butterfly effect is applicable to our job histories: the experiences and contacts we gain from one employer may influence our next work assignment in unseen ways. The stark truth is that none of us can predict the future or anticipate how our current jobs may impact our eventual career paths. No one is more aware of the serendipity of seemingly unconnected events than Jeffrey Katzenberg.

After Katzenberg's junior year of high school, he volunteered to work in the office of Mayor John Lindsay in New York. The experience proved beneficial to Katzenberg as it pointed him toward working with New York producer and studio executive John Picker, the first of his major influences. As Katzenberg related in his 2008 Ringling College speech, "I assure you that when I started out as a gofer in the New York mayor's office, it did not occur to me that this would send me on my path to becoming a Hollywood studio executive. Each of you is going to have your own career path and, chances are, since you have chosen a career in the arts, your path is likely to be highly unpredictable. So, don't be afraid to take the first step because *you never know.*"

As rewarding and satisfying as my days on *Roger Rabbit* were, the film itself soon took a back seat to an even greater opportunity. Because the film was a co-production between Walt Disney Productions and Amblin Entertain-

Production Manager on *Goofy* TV special

Production Manager on *Richard Dreyfuss Project*

Production Coordinator on *Roger Rabbit*

Producer at Amblimation

Director at DreamWorks, *The Prince of Egypt*

ment, being part of the movie's crew allowed me contact with the talented Amblin nucleus of Robert Zemeckis, Robert Watts, Kathleen Kennedy, Frank Marshall, and Steven Spielberg. Fortunately for me, I was able to make a favorable enough impression so that sixteen months later, I was hired to help set up Spielberg's new feature animation unit, Amblimation.

It was an implausible but relatively straight three-year trajectory from my agreeing to help salvage a troubled twenty-one-minute Goofy short to my role as being a producer on a Steven Spielberg animated film. And from my work as a producer for Spielberg in London, I was offered the chance to direct *The Prince of Egypt* when Steven Spielberg, Jeffrey Katzenberg, and David Geffen formed DreamWorks Studios.

If I had said "No" just once, I may have missed major career opportunities.

WHEN OPPORTUNITY KNOCKS, RUN—DON'T WALK—TO ANSWER THE DOOR

If you get the chance to upgrade your skills, take it! In the early years of my career, I knew several artists who bemoaned the fact that they "never got the breaks" that others did. But the truth was that they had the same opportunities as their more successful peers—they simply made the wrong choices.

One striking example of a co-worker missing out on a life-changing opportunity happened during the shift from traditional, hand-drawn animation to computer animation. After the success of *Toy Story*, the artist was offered the chance to learn how to animate on the computer (while getting paid)—but turned it down. Now years later, the jobs in feature animation field are for computer-savvy artists, and he has had difficulty finding work.

Sometimes you need to create your own breaks. Usually, the only way you will get the chance to move into a great new position is if you are already proficient in your current capacity. Let us assume that you have been with a company for some time and you are recognized as being a hardworking, upbeat employee; what is the next step?

ASK FOR OPPORTUNITY, NOT MONEY

Some animators seek immediate gratification over future benefit. These misdirected people would choose short-term gain over a long-term investment in themselves. At Amblimation's London studio, I would often have artists come to my office asking for  a raise. My philosophy, on the other hand, has always been that when you are ready to call in your favors, you need to make sure that what you are asking for will pay off in the biggest possible way. *Ask for the chance to improve yourself instead of asking for money.*

The problem with specifically requesting a raise in salary is that you are not substantially improving your long-term situation. If you win the increase in pay, what happens? You get a bit more money, you can buy a few more things, and perhaps your standard of living is higher—but those rewards are short-term. The reality is you have not improved your prospects. Soon you will find yourself dissatisfied again because, for most people, money alone does not elicit job fulfillment. True job satisfaction comes from doing work that challenges you and brings out your best.

On the other hand, when you ask your employer for an opportunity, you appear proactive. You are showing him/her that you want to improve yourself so that you can better serve him/her. Asking for money puts the employer in an awkward position, but seeking opportunity does not obligate him/her. In this situation, the employer has every incentive to help you; he/she can see you are trying to further contribute to the company. Asking for opportunity is about looking for career growth, and career growth will bring both money and further job satisfaction.

THE TWO MINUTES OF TIME RULE

While I was working on Dreyfuss' Constitution TV special, Don Hahn, one of my mentors at Disney, had relocated to London to serve as the animation producer on *Roger Rabbit*. Several months into production, the movie was turning out to be more difficult than expected. The technique that Robert Zemeckis (the film's director), Richard Wil-

liams (the animation director), and Ken Ralston (the visual effects supervisor) had created was groundbreaking, but it required virtually every shot in the movie to be created three times: once in live action, once in animation, and finally with the two elements composited together at George Lucas' Industrial Light and Magic effects studio. To the producers and the filmmakers, the process was the equivalent of making three movies at once, and they were falling behind their anticipated summer 1988 release date.

Word traveled in the animation community that the studio might be starting a second unit for *Roger Rabbit* in Los Angeles. Armed with the latest rumor, I decided to approach Peter Schneider, the vice president in charge of Disney Feature Animation. I picked my moment carefully—choosing a time after work when I knew his assistant would have left, and he would be alone in his office. I knew that he would be busy, so I asked if I could have just two minutes of his time. (Lee Bobker, one of my New York University instructors—and a successful documentary producer—told me, "No one is so busy that they can't spare you two minutes!") Once Schneider granted me my two minutes, I went into my speech. "Peter," I said, "I've worked on two projects that nobody else wanted to do, and now I've heard that there might be an L.A. unit for *Roger Rabbit*. I don't know if it's true, but if there is a unit, I would like to be considered." That was my whole pitch.

Schneider could not let me leave with such a tantalizing subject hanging in the air. He asked what I had heard about *Roger Rabbit* creating a Los Angeles unit to take the pressure off the London studio. I replied to Schneider that I had not heard any specific news beyond the vague hearsay around the studio that a small unit was being considered. Schneider replied that there was discussion of another unit, but that nothing definite had been decided upon. I thanked Schneider for his time, and left his office. The entire discussion lasted just a few minutes.

Within a week, I was the second person hired for the *Roger Rabbit* Los Angeles unit.

Within two months, I was packing up my apartment and heading to London to join Don Hahn at the main *Roger Rabbit* studio. To this day, I owe Peter Schneider and Don Hahn a great deal of gratitude for assigning me to the film, *Who Framed Roger Rabbit?* Without their support and guidance, I would never have had the career break that forever changed my life.

Several years later I would make another request for an opportunity that would lead me to another career course change.

Balto was the third film produced at the Amblimation London studio, and it was based on the true account of the 1925 diphtheria epidemic in Nome, Alaska. Unfortunately for the infirmed of Nome, the only available antitoxin was in Anchorage—a city besieged by a blizzard and whose only aircraft was inoperable. With mounting casualties, the choice was made to send a sled team to deliver the serum with the head dog, Balto. Balto and his team succeeded, and today the Iditarod commemorates the historic journey of the sled team. Our animated film told this real-life tale of heroism from the point of view of anthropomorphic sled dogs and their friend, a Russian goose.

During the production of *Balto*, the decision was made to move Amblimation Studios from London back to Los Angeles where the artists would have greater access to Steven Spielberg. The experience of working on *Balto* was wonderful and I enjoyed the chance to contribute to the story. Being involved on such a creative level stimulated the artistic side within me again, and I started to think that I would like to try my hand at directing an animated movie. At the time, I had been working in an assortment of production roles for almost seven years, and I had not been drawing on a daily basis for all that time.

The move back to Los Angeles seemed to be a great opportunity. One afternoon when Bonne Radford, the animation executive for Amblin, was visiting London from her Universal City office, I made the second of my life-changing pitches. As I spoke, I mentioned that I would like to be considered as a director if a film in development seemed to be a good fit for me. Once again, my whole potentially career-altering pitch lasted only a couple of minutes. At that time, there was not a particular film in development that I was lobbying for, but rather I was planting the idea of the studio seeing me as a potential director.

Radford agreed that I would be a good choice for a director. With her support, I was hired by Universal Pictures as one of three directors on an animated version of the Andrew Lloyd Webber hit musical, *Cats*. As fate would have it, within a couple of months, Amblimation was absorbed into a new company, DreamWorks, and I was lucky to be chosen to co-direct *The Prince of Egypt* with *Balto's* director, Simon Wells, and Brenda Chapman, the head of story from Disney's *The Lion King*. (*Cats* as an animated property stayed with Universal Pictures until Lloyd Webber decided to release a DVD of the filmed musical.)

BE PATIENT FOR THE PAYOFF

Each time I asked for a specific opportunity (the first time, to work on *Roger Rabbit*, the second time, to direct), I had already invested a great deal of time in the company, working without complaint. Before I went to Peter Schneider to test the possibility of joining the *Roger Rabbit* crew, I had spent over a year and a half helping to keep two television productions on track. During that time,

I spent a lot of Saturdays and late nights making sure that both productions did not require too much attention from the Disney production executives. Nothing is worse for a company than when a low-priority project goes off the rails and requires heavy supervision and allocation of important resources. When I decided to float the idea of directing to Amblin executive Bonne Radford, I had been working for the company for four years as an animation producer. Because of the eight-hour time difference between Los Angeles and London, all the Amblin executives were aware of how many long nights our production crew had been working.

Once you have proven yourself and you believe the timing is correct, ask for the opportunity to move to the next level. Trust that when you take the step, you will get the money and compensation you deserve. Asking for opportunity—and not money—will help you achieve a more rewarding career.

TO BE THE BEST SURROUND YOURSELF WITH THE BEST

My high school had two bands, and the premiere band with the best musicians was called the "A" band. If you still wanted to play in a band but were not proficient enough for the "A" band, you could join the "B" band. But even to a high school kid one thing was clear: the best way to improve was to make sure that you were in the group with the most talented people. I realized back then that it was preferable to be the weakest guy on the best team, rather than the best guy on a weaker team.

Along with the approach of "Asking for Opportunity, Not Money," attaching yourself to first-rate talent is one of the best ways to ensure a great career trajectory. I have seen many fellow artists join up with lesser-quality studios because they got to be departmental top-dogs, only to watch the studio fizzle and leave the artist with a weak mark on his/her resume. Meanwhile, the guy who worked at the top-notch studio, in perhaps a lesser capacity, walked away from his job with cachet. In business—especially Hollywood—there is no better career currency than working on a successful product. By following the talent, you will improve faster in your job, gain greater job satisfaction, and protect your career longevity.

3

GETTING THE BREAKS
AND MAKING THEM HAPPEN

*"If you're not failing every now and again,
it's a sign you're not doing anything very innovative."*
—Woody Allen

When I started at DreamWorks Animation in 1995, there was a project in development based on a slim children's book with an odd title that translated to "fear" in German. The original thought was to animate the movie using a combination of frame-by-frame computer animation, and a then-new approach called motion capture technology. The technique for motion capture consisted of putting an actor in a suit covered with sensors. As the performer acted out the scene, the computer recorded the movements, thus capturing the performance. The next step would be to take the digital information that had been recorded and allow a computer artist to animate the dialogue using "replacement animation," a stop-motion animation technique that uses pre-formed mouth shapes. The hybrid of motion capture and replacement animation did not prove as successful as the filmmaking team had hoped, and the technique was abandoned in favor of a traditional computer animation approach where the computer animator would pose out the acting using three-dimensional computer models of the character in frame-by-frame fashion.

While the technicians were struggling with the technical aspects of the movie, the storytellers were running into difficulties defining the personality of the lead character. Finally, the filmmakers hit upon a gold mine when they signed the terrific comedian Chris Farley for the title role. Somehow Farley's bigger-than-life personality, coupled with his ability to soften the edges of the movie's crude humor, worked perfectly, and the studio had their green ogre. The character's name was Shrek.

Then, just as the movie was finally taking shape, tragedy struck. On December 18, 1997, comedian Chris Farley met an untimely death. The crew of *Shrek* was stunned by the terrible loss, and everyone wondered if the film would ever be finished. After all, everyone could see that the main character of Shrek only started to work when Chris Farley joined the movie, and the crew was filled with the fear that the hard knock had set them back to the beginning. The legacy of what was to become DreamWorks' signature property could have ended there had it not been for the astute observations of Jeffrey Katzenberg.

The loss of Chris Farley was devastating, but Katzenberg reasoned that over the past months, the story and tone of *Shrek* had been set. Although recreating the Chris Farley version of the character Shrek would be impossible, Katzenberg felt that another actor might be able to take the role and give the green ogre his own particular spin. After a respectful period of grieving, a search yielded another master of comedy, Mike Myers. The pairing of Mike Myers with Eddie Murphy as Donkey proved irresistible, and the movie became an enormous worldwide hit. Instead of being overwhelmed by misfortune, Katzenberg assessed that the project could be resuscitated, and his judgment was rewarded with the creation of one of Hollywood's most successful franchises.

TURN SETBACKS INTO STEPPING STONES

Setbacks are only temporary; the misfortune of today may be a push into a new direction for tomorrow.

The four guys who performed that unsuccessful test on motion capture technology on *Shrek* were part of a company called PropellerHead Design. They rebounded from their setback and moved on to other projects. Loren Soman and Andy Waisler worked on such hits as *I, Robot; Aeon Flux*; and *Basic Instinct*. Another member of the team, Rob  Letterman, became a successful writer/director on *Shark Tale, Monsters vs. Aliens,* and *Gulliver's Travels.* And the last of the crewmembers? He elected to change his credit from "Jeffrey" to "J. J.," and as J. J. Abrams, went on to create the popular television shows *Felicity, Alias, Lost,* and *Fringe*, to direct *Mission Impossible III,* and to oversee the rebooting of the *Star Trek* and *Star Wars* franchises.

Creative industries are often cyclical. Bad times will return, and how you respond to the lean stretches in your life will determine how well you are situated in the future. In 1982 there was a great turndown in the animation business, and many people were out of work. I worked a scant ten weeks that entire year. Out of those dire times, however, came my realization that I needed to raise my skill level. Although the job market was horrendous for a while, the personal inventory I took and the positive path I chose has kept me consistently employed for over twenty-five years.

The key factor in transforming your setbacks into opportunities is that you must be open-minded enough to analyze what has allowed you to fall into your unfortunate position. You need to take some responsibility for your own situation. When I was out of work for a long stretch, I was aware that some of my colleagues were working. By keeping an open mind, I admitted that my drawing skills were not as strong as those of my peers. I could see that their advanced abilities made them more employable. Instead of blaming my unemployed status on the studios sending work overseas for cheaper labor costs, I used my free time to take more drawing classes and reinvent myself as a better artist.

RECOGNIZE A GREAT OPPORTUNITY

Great opportunities are out there, but they require you to recognize them and then profit from them. I have worked twice in what were considered terrible workspaces, and both times those crazy, castoff locations placed me in the path of career breakthroughs.

Before Spider-Man and Optimus Prime became computer-generated heroes, animators most often worked with pencil and paper. The artists would draw loose versions of their characters' actions, called "roughs," and then hand their scenes to be pencil tested. The pencil tester worked with a camera mounted on an upright stand that was capable of capturing one frame at a time. In order to film the scene of finished animation, the tester would place each drawing (or set of drawings) onto a set of registration pegs, and shoot the frames individually. When all the drawings in the scene had been shot in succession, the work could be viewed in real time for approval. In the early days of animation, these test cameras used film, but in the seventies, video recorders became commonplace and studios adopted this faster—and cheaper—technology.

Shooting video pencil tests was my first job in animation,

and—although I did not know it then—my placement in the department was a situation of being at the right place at the right time. The job enabled me to have access to every animator at the studio, and as a bonus, I was situated across the hall from the producer. The workload for the department was heavy, and I found myself working overtime most nights. Overtime is endemic to the entertainment business, and I have always remembered the advice of NYU Professor Lee Bobker, who said that filmmaking was not a job or a career—rather, it was a lifestyle. You had to love movies because working in entertainment would mean a lot of long days.

Filmation's producer, Don Christensen, would meander into the video room after normal working hours to view the latest work, and his visits became a ritual. He would grab a soft drink and set himself down in front of the monitor while I played back the day's animation footage. I was never one to miss an opportunity to talk film, and so, as the clips ran on the monitor, I would tell Christensen about the latest movies that I had seen. There was rarely a new release that I had not seen. Because I was so familiar with current movies, I became Christensen's resident critic. As it turned out, Christensen was also a huge student of film, especially old movies, and we would often end the sessions talking about some classic movie we both loved. So there I was, chatting each night with the producer for every show produced by Filmation Studios—all from a job that my predecessor video testers could not wait to leave. I was harvesting a great deal of goodwill, and my familiarity with Christensen afforded me chances that I would not have had otherwise.

During my free time, I was writing a speculative script for a new television series, *Sport Billy,* which was in pre-production. I had designs on moving into the writing department, and since I was having daily discussions with the studio's producer, I felt that I could venture to show him my work. To my delight, Christensen found my script funny, but because the writing department was under the leadership of Arthur Nadel, the vice president of creative affairs, he thought that my best chance to influence the stories was in the storyboard department.

Sport Billy was being produced for broadcast on German television and involved the adventures of a time-traveling boy and girl and their talking dog. Fortunately for me, *Sport Billy* was a cartoony show as opposed to the naturalistic action adventure shows that Filmation usually produced. The fact that the characters were easier to draw masked one of my darkest secrets: I had no training in how to create functioning storyboards for a studio such as Filmation. As the days went by, I managed to draw the characters proficiently, but I was experiencing difficulties in telling the story in both an entertaining and economic way. Because Filmation kept all their work stateside, the studio required the board artists to contain the amount of animation required in order to rein in costs. However, I was having such trouble telling the story that my storyboards were becoming complicated. Among life's miseries, trying to tread water in a job where you are underqualified must be at the top of the heap. When the time came for the first review of my storyboards, the massive shortfalls in my job competence were apparent.

Karl Geurs, the teddy bear of a man who was in charge of the department, did his best to let me down gently, but I was gutted. Worst of all, I figured that since I was being fired from the storyboard department, I would be back on the street  without work. What I could not have foreseen was how supportive Filmation Studios would be as a company. Led by Lou Scheimer, a man of great integrity and conviction, Filmation took care of their people. Long-time employees headed up most departments in the company, and there was a deep sense of loyalty among the leadership.

Although I was told that my storyboards were not at the level the studio required, Karl Geurs told me that my old job was still available. When I heard the news, I practically danced down the hallway to my former office, happy that I had been saved from the unemployment line. In returning to my previous role as a video pencil tester, I was blissfully unaware that I was setting in motion my phoenix-like rise from the ashes.

Despite my demotion, Don Christensen still viewed me as a story person—not a pencil tester. And this change in perception worked to my advantage when Christensen soon found himself running into trouble. In reviewing the storyboards for the shows in production, he had suggestions for improvements that he wanted implemented. Unfortunately, the story artists were swamped with work and no one was available for the revisions. No one, that is, except for the recently demoted storyboard artist who was fortuitously situated across the hall from him.

Me.

And so began my apprenticeship in the world of storyboard revisions. Christensen would hand me rough drawings of his suggested storyboard fixes, and I would do tighter drawings for the final image. Over the subsequent weeks, his rough drawings gave way to detailed notes, and eventually he would just hand me the storyboard and ask me to rework certain elements. By the end of the TV season, I was no longer doing revisions; I was back in the storyboard department—and this time I stayed.

Several pencil testers preceded me and several others would follow, but I do not think anyone took better advantage of the job than I did. Virtually everyone who stepped into that small room to shoot pencil tests saw the work as a stopgap job, a temporary position before they jumped into the animation pool. I never viewed the role in such terms. Shooting pencil tests provided me with access to dozens of talented artists and directors, as well as the studio's producer. My enthusiasm for the job allowed me to benefit much more from the situation than any of my predecessors.

Several years after my first job as a pencil tester, I was sent to London to work on *Who Framed Roger Rabbit?* I came onto the film during the final crunch period when the studio was short on space. The crew had grown manyfold from the initial projections and people were working anywhere there was room to squeeze in a desk. By November 1987, the only available workplace was the studio's theater, a dark, dank room that was filled in the mornings with crewmembers viewing the latest finished footage. Each day when the room emptied after the third showing of dailies, a noticeable stench of body odor lingered. The conditions were less than ideal, and everyone commiserated with me about having to work in such a dreadful environment. The truth was quite the opposite: I was the luckiest guy on the movie.

Although I had to put up with a certain amount of disagreeable air, there were some significant advantages. At some point during each day, every member of the crew passed through my "office." The list included Frank Marshall and Robert Watts, the producers; Robert Zemeckis, the director; Richard Williams, the animation director; Don Hahn, Disney's outstanding animation producer; and Steve Starkey and Ken Ralston, the Industrial Light and Magic effects geniuses. On special occasions, I would see Jeffrey Katzenberg, Disney's head of motion pictures; Peter Schneider, Disney's animation chief; George Lucas; Steven Spielberg; and even once, the Muppets' creator, Jim Henson. That smelly room turned out to be one of the greatest gathering grounds for movie talent imaginable—and I was right in the middle of it! By the end of my months in London, I had made enough of a favorable impression on Frank Marshall and Robert Watts that a year later they offered me a job as associate producer for Steven Spielberg's new animation studio in London. When I hear people complain about not getting breaks, I think about my time spent in the *Roger Rabbit* screening room.

And I am not the only one to benefit from working in less than ideal conditions. George Lucas described the first office at Lucas Computer Graphics for John Lasseter, who later became the creative founder of Pixar, as being very unassuming. "We put John in a little closet. Literally, a closet."

No one can promise you a ticket to success. But learn everything you can about the job you are doing, and situate yourself so that you can make your own opportunities.

4

DO IT NOW, NOT LATER

"Procrastination is opportunity's assassin."
—Victor Kiam

In Walt Disney's adaptation of *Sleeping Beauty*, the evil queen Maleficent places a curse on the baby princess Aurora. The spell dictates that Aurora will die when she pricks her finger on a spinning wheel. Before this blight takes effect, one of the benevolent fairies tempers the curse so that the princess will not die—but will sleep. As you know, Sleeping Beauty and her prince overcome the spell and live "happily ever after." Unfortunately for us, such stories are make-believe. When we make mistakes, we are forced to live with the consequences of our actions. But reflecting upon the tale of *Sleeping Beauty* got me wondering about real-life scourges; what malady would I inflict upon a person if I wanted to damn him/her to a life of underachievement?

The answer to my question came quickly. By imbuing my victim with one simple personality flaw, I could make certain that he/she would live a life of unfulfilled promise. I would make him/her a procrastinator.

JOIN THE "DO IT NOW" SOCIETY

If ever there were a Hall of Fame for "doing it now," Jeffrey Katzenberg would be elected on the first ballot. In the decade-plus that I have worked with Katzenberg, I can honestly say that I have never seen anyone who attacks a task with greater imperative. And his appetite for results extends to those around him. Whenever there is the expectation that a job will be completed the next day, you can be certain that you will be receiving a call promptly asking when he can see the results. Katzenberg likes to move quickly, and it is exhilarating to work in such an environment.

Katzenberg is one of the top practitioners of the "do it now" philosophy, but he is not alone in subscribing to this work method. Think of any successful person you know. In all likelihood, that person has the habit of attacking tasks immediately, rather than putting things off.

PROCRASTINATION: THE SILENT CAREER KILLER

I do not believe there is an easier habit to acquire than procrastination. The trait is seductive and the rewards are compelling. We get to put off doing an unappealing task for the pleasure of immediate fun. Who wants to  study for that economics test when there is a party down the hall? One may think, "This business report will wait until I finish filling out the bowl games pool." I plead guilty to the draw of procrastination. It is a cruel trick of fate that allows the machine that I use to write to be the same device that I can use to shop, search for sports scores, and check e-mail. Procrastination is one of the single most self-destructive traits we can possess.

I have known many terrific artists who are big procrastinators, and that single trait has dampened the types of assignments they receive. I worked with one gifted artist on a project, but his tendency to delay stopped me from giving him the best assignments. On too many occasions, he would hand in his material late—or at the last moment. By being overdue with his work, he effectively eliminated my opportunity to make sure all the parts of the job blended together as best they could. The artist's refusal to be on time affected the type of work he received. His habit of procrastinating hampered his career growth.

Time was critical during my years working on television animation at Filmation Studios. In television, as opposed to feature film animation, airdates arrive on a weekly basis. Procrastination can be terminal. I worked with one excellent artist who seemed incapable of using his time well. He was chronically late with his work, and eventually he had not only poisoned his name at Filmation, but within a few years, he had missed so many deadlines he had become virtually unemployable. Continual late performance will result in a stagnant career, or being marginalized within the industry.

ANTI-PROCRASTINATION TIPS

The good news for procrastinators is that once they get over the initial resistance to beginning a task, they usually become committed to their work. Here are a few tricks to help you stop procrastinating.

1   Make the reward for beginning the task more enticing than whatever you are doing to avoid it. Make a pact with yourself that when you complete a prescribed amount of your task, you will go for a walk, a swim, or whatever will motivate you (which will be far more interesting than whatever you are doing to procrastinate —i.e., surfing the Internet). The key aspect of this whole self-deception is to encourage yourself to begin. Once you are invested in a job, it's easier to keep going. It is the early resistance that is the hurdle you must overcome.

2 Make beginning the job a competition with yourself. This works for me since I am a natural-born competitor. I create my own mini-deadline and then I try to finish more than I am anticipating in the time frame. I find that turning the task that I am eschewing into a contest gives me the push I need at the outset. Sometimes the best approach for breaking through work delay tactics is to create some physical activity that will serve as a precursor to beginning the task. The action might be as simple as brushing your teeth after lunch, taking a walk around the office (walking up and down stairs is useful for this), making a cup of coffee, or just stepping outside for some fresh air. Whatever enterprise you choose, be sure to avoid "rabbit hole" activities such as making phone calls or answering e-mails, as they can co-opt your energy and become time thieves.

3 When I find myself unusually resistant to a task, I induce myself to begin by lowering my expectations. For instance, if I feel I should work out on my elliptical trainer but I do not have the desire, I tell myself that I will exercise for only five minutes. Once I overcome my initial barrier, I find that I am open to continuing. And so, my five-minute pledge may grow to half an hour.

LEAVE SOMETHING FUN FOR TOMORROW

Procrastination in the world of the professional writer is so ubiquitous that they have coined a euphemism for it: "writer's block." Neil Simon, the great playwright, spoke  at a writer's seminar I attended, and one of the audience members asked him if he ever found himself unable to get started in the morning. Simon replied that he did not suffer from that malady. He said that he had developed a trick to avoid the usual inertia of getting started each day. He always stopped the day's writing just before he reached an exciting place in the story. By employing this technique, Simon found that he knew exactly what he was going to write the next morning and discovered that he was eager to resume his work.

Simon's work method proved to be a lightning bolt for me. I now apply his secret to any long-term task. When I know that I am getting close to the end of the workday, I will pause just before I get to a natural stopping point. Then, just as Simon described, I find it easier to begin work the next morning. I know exactly where I will begin, and I overcome any resistance to starting a new workday by finishing off the prior day's work.

EGO

The word *ego* is Latin for "I." And if there is one thing that Hollywood has in greater supply than talent, it is ego. The entertainment business is difficult, highly competitive, and crazy, and having a strong ego is a requisite for success. Without a reasonable belief in one's own abilities, it would be impossible for an actor to audition, a writer to pour out her feelings in a speculative script, or a musician to submit a demo tape. But the need to toot your own horn is not limited to Hollywood. Anyone who fills out an application with a hope of landing a job, or interviews with a roomful of human resource professionals, knows how vulnerable we can feel. In order to win that coveted job or attract the attention of a mate, we need to have some sense of confidence, which comes from our ego.

A healthy ego is necessary, but when a person's ego becomes his/her dominant motivator, trouble may arise. Robert M. Pirsig in his seminal book, *Zen and the Art of Motorcycle Maintenance*, described the danger of allowing one's ego to drive the hunger for success:

> "Any effort that has self-glorification as its final endpoint is bound to end in disaster."

When someone focuses on the expectation of accolades rather than the enjoyment of the work process, that person is setting up himself for disappointment. The ego-driven worker is a bottomless well of neediness, and no amount of admiration and attention will be enough.

Egotism is not confined to individuals. Sometimes an entire corporate culture will be infected with the "I did this" mentality. I never realized how divisive such a culture could be—where everyone feels compelled to claim credit for their work—until I worked at a place where those sensibilities were absent. After a string of when-I-did-this companies, I was hired by Steven Spielberg's Amblin Entertainment, and within a matter of days, I noticed that everyone at the company substituted the word "we" for "I." The difference between the Amblin culture and every other company where I had worked was profound. At Amblin, I heard phrases such as, "We can do this," "This is what we are thinking," and, "We can work on this." I fell in love with the company because I felt that at Amblin, all of us were working together as a group. Furthermore, there was no sense of me, as a newly hired person, being an outsider compared to the long-term Amblin employees. I felt that all of us would share in the company's success and resolve any problems together. Amblin was a studio of inclusion where everyone contributed ideas.

Nearly six years at Spielberg's animation studio trained me to downplay my ego in favor of an inclusive creative environment. By choosing to use "we" instead of "I," everyone at Amblin reinforced the idea that the filmmaking process was a group effort. When much of the Amblimation studio was later incorporated into DreamWorks Animation, I was happy to see that the new company embraced the "we" mentality. I have now worked for so many years within an inclusive culture that whenever I do hear a worker claim individual credit, I react with surprise. I know that she is just taking one more step toward self-glorification and that ultimately will fall prey to great disappointment.

5

MENTORS, AND WORKING IN CIRCLES

"The best teacher is not the one who knows most but the one who is most capable of reducing knowledge to that simple compound of the obvious and wonderful."
—H.L. Mencken

When I moved to Los Angeles after graduating from New York University, I had no connections in the movie business. In a town where the saying, "It's not what you know, it's who you know," is not just a collection of words, but a modus operandi, I was at a disadvantage. Thankfully, I was naïve beyond all measure, and I figured that if I knocked on enough doors, someone would eventually let me in. With a 16mm projector and a film in hand, I paraded to the studios in Los Angeles. Absolute dumb luck was with me the day that I called upon Filmation Studios in Reseda and asked if anyone would be willing to take a look at my animated student film. On that day, I found my first mentor.

The man who looked at my work was Karran (Kay) Wright,

and he ended up being my guardian angel for my early years in the animation business. By coincidence, he was born in the same year as my father and he looked after me as if I were his son. At the time of my interview with Wright, there were no openings that fit my very limited skill set, so he took my number and promised to call when there was a vacancy. A month later, true to his word, Wright gave me the job that started my career in animation.

Three years after I met Wright, the country was in a major recession and the animation business was in turmoil. The studios were in the process of sending more work overseas, and the available job pool became negligible. I was underexperienced and underqualified, and by this time, Wright had moved to another studio. My bank account was disappearing faster than the Incredible Shrinking Man when suddenly, I received a call offering me work. It was Kay Wright coming to my rescue.

Wright had one of those resumes worthy of Forrest Gump—wherever history was taking place, he seemed to be part of it. He started in the animation business back when Disney was making a little film called *Snow White and the Seven Dwarfs*, but he later left the studio in order to make the rank of character animator. Along the way, he worked at most of the landmark studios, including Hanna-Barbera, when it pioneered television animation. During our time together, Wright told me stories about Disney during the golden age, and demonstrated how they had achieved the brilliant water effects in *Pinocchio* and the magic mirror effect in *Snow White*. I soaked it all up. It was as if I had a living reference book divulging to me its contents.

Years later, I was producing for Amblimation in London when a friend forwarded me Wright's phone number. When I called Wright, he was surprised—he did not imagine that I would remember him. I told Wright that I could never forget him; I owed him an immense debt of gratitude for helping me. As we chatted, I could tell that he was pleased that I was doing well in animation. At the end of the call I told Wright that I could never repay him for all the good that he had done for me; the only thing that I could do was to one day help someone as he had done for me.

Despite its reputation, the movie business is full of selfless mentor relationships. Oscar-winning film composer Hans Zimmer was mentored by Stanley Myers, and has, in turn, mentored a succession of newer generation film composers—whose credits include the biggest hits of today. As Zimmer has demonstrated, the only true way to repay a mentor is by "paying it forward" to each succeeding generation.

The mentor/student relationship takes different forms, and with each of my mentors we somehow drifted together into the same orbit. I never set out  to attach myself to any leader. It happened naturally. In retrospect, I believe that my curiosity for moviemaking drew me to certain supervisors, and by coming back to solicit advice and learn from them, we made a connection. I cannot imagine any business relationship as enriching for both parties as the mentor/student one. To me, there are two components necessary to catch the interest of a mentor. First, there must be sufficient contact to build a relationship. Nowadays, e-mail and social media allow a person enough familiarity that he/she can create a mentor-student relationship through cyberspace. Of course, there is no substitute for daily personal contact, but I do think that a newcomer can learn quite a bit from an experienced worker through written communications. Second—and perhaps most importantly—the student must be harder working and more committed to his/her field than his/her peers. It is crucial that you do not just appear to be interested. *Be* interested! People who are masters at their jobs can sense a charlatan.

For a mentor, there is nothing more exciting than having an exceptional talent to tutor. I have thought about what has drawn me to particular "new-to-animation" hires and the answer is the same: I am looking for someone who has that same fire and love of movies/animation that I have. My most valuable commodity in life is time, and I want to feel that my effort will be worthwhile. The price of admission to a mentor-student relationship is that the talent-in-the-making must do his/her homework. I enjoy feeling challenged by a new student and when I sense that he has invested in himself, I am eager to help him become his best.

Both Steven Spielberg and Jeffrey Katzenberg have voiced appreciation for the help they received from their selfless mentors. For Steven Spielberg, Sid Sheinberg, chief operating officer for MCA/Universal, was instrumental in discovering him and nurturing his career. Later, Steve Ross, CEO for Time Warner, had such an influence on Spielberg that the film *Schindler's List* is dedicated to him.

Jeffrey Katzenberg considers himself to have gained from the experiences of many individuals, but there have always been special mentors for him. The first of them, David Picker, a New York producer and executive, not only eased Katzenberg into the world of moviemaking, but also performed the ultimate selfless act by urging him to fly to Los Angeles and interview with Barry Diller, who was then the CEO of Paramount Pictures. Diller would become the second of Katzenberg's mentors, and Katzenberg credits Diller for creating an environment of "Hollywood concentrate," where he was tutored in the nuts and bolts of moviemaking in a compressed period.

The third of Katzenberg's mentors was the most unusual—because by the time Katzenberg studied under him, Walt Disney had been dead for nearly two decades. Although Disney was no longer at the studio when Katzenberg arrived there in 1984, the studio's archives were bursting with detailed story notes and accounts of the visionary's moviemaking process. As Katzenberg recalled in his 2008 speech, "...it was as if he left breadcrumbs the size of Volkswagens." Walt Disney had a huge impact on Katzenberg, infusing him with a new passion in his career—animation. Over the years, Katzenberg has been a mentor for many in Hollywood, and he has never ceased to be an advocate for this memorable type of relationship. Speaking of mentors to a class of college seniors, Katzenberg said, "Find them. Appreciate them. And appreciate their encouragement of you and make sure you earn it."

FIND THE "ONE THING" IN YOUR JOB

In the comedy *City Slickers*, there is a moment where Jack Palance's character, Curly, holds up a finger and declares that "one thing" is the secret to living a happy life. Desperate for the answer to life's mysteries, Mitch (Billy Crystal), one of the weekend cowboys, asks what that "one thing" is. With a rhetorical hint to his voice, Curly replies, "That's what you have to find out."

I had a similar moment one afternoon when I slipped into Glen Keane's office. At the time, the Disney animation department was in a deep funk; we had just completed *The Great Mouse Detective*, which failed to make an impact at the box office. The next project was a retelling of the classic Dickens story, *Oliver Twist,* except told through the eyes of stray cats and dogs in modern day New York City. To say that the artists were underwhelmed would be charitable. Most of the staff was not looking forward to working two years on what they considered to be a retread of a tired story.

Keane's room was different.

There was a sense of excitement and the promise of great opportunity. While many of the artists were grousing about the lackluster premise, expressive drawings and terrific shots of animation were exploding off Keane's desk. This guy was not bored with his job. He was attacking the assignment with the thrill of an artist handed a pencil for the first time. Personally, I could not imagine what he was finding so exhilarating about his work, and I had to ask him how he managed to be so enthusiastic.

He told me that every job, every assignment that he received was an opportunity to improve—and a chance to gain a skill that he did not already possess. Keane explained that his paper and pencil were all the tools that he needed to become a better artist. Most importantly, he said that when he sat down to start a movie, he picked one thing he wanted to learn by the end of the film—and by selecting that one thing, he ensured that he was challenged on a daily basis. And since he was constantly being challenged, he couldn't help but be excited by his work. Keane had found life's magic recipe, and with that "one thing," he would embrace whatever challenge was given to him.

What Keane taught me that day was that the restrictions of my enthusiasm were in my head. The excitement of a task is not inherent in the job; the stimulation is inside the person. When I realized that I could learn something new and become better-skilled every time I was handed a job, I discovered that I no longer had a problem finding enthusiasm.

Keane's dedication to "personal best" was infectious, and he always had a group of hopefuls vying to be part of his unit. Somehow his crew always seemed to be doing the best work on a film. To Keane, every task was another opportunity to expand his skill set, and his ability to share his quest for learning is what made him a superlative mentor.

Listening to Keane speak, I was reminded of the quote often attributed to Stanislavski, a teacher of method acting, who said: "There are no small parts, only small actors."

6

BReaKING THROUGH aND MOVING UP

"The secret of getting ahead is getting started"
—Mark Twain

There is one question I never tire of hearing the answer to: "How did you break into the movie business?" No matter how many people I ask, I always get a compelling reply. One colleague told me that when he first moved to Los Angeles, he was so short of money that he snuck into Universal Studios and lived in one of the houses on the back lot. He regaled me with adventures of his having to duck behind the windows every time he heard one of the tour trams rumble past "his house."

Another friend told me that he got a job at a local pizzeria because he learned that a particular sound studio where he wished to work often ordered pizzas from the restaurant. By delivering pizzas to the studio in the evenings, he became friendly with the sound crew and was later hired.

One artist I know built a stop-motion *Tyrannosaurus rex*

model (in those pre-computer days) and took it to an animation studio hoping for work. When they told him they only were hiring animators who could draw, he bluffed his way into a training program.

These are all great "How I Got Started" stories, but my favorite one comes from George Clooney. I heard Clooney tell his tale at a post-screening discussion for his movie, *The Ides of March,* where much of the audience was comprised of actors. One young woman talked about her struggles to get a foothold in the industry and wondered if Clooney had any advice. He responded that most people think he became an overnight success when he landed his life-changing role on *E.R.,* but that was far from the truth. "People weren't there when I was living in a friend's closet, and they weren't there when I couldn't get an audition," Clooney said. He admitted that when he finally started to get noticed, he still had *fifteen* failed TV pilots before he clicked with *E.R.*

At the time when his phone wasn't ringing, Clooney had a friend who was a receptionist at a talent agency. She was privy to all the roles being cast and she passed on the list to Clooney. But even with the names of the production companies and acting parts available, he could not secure an audition without being recommended from an agent.

So "Josh Reynolds" was born. As agent "Josh Reynolds," Clooney would call the production companies and give laudatory recommendations to the casting departments for his "client," Clooney himself. At the end of the call, "Josh Reynolds" would leave the phone number for the agency where his friend worked, and when the casting department would later contact the agency, she would call her friend George at his apartment and connect them. The ruse worked, and from then on, Clooney was never short of audition opportunities.

SUCCESS TAKES TIME

One day while we were making *Bee Movie*, Jerry Seinfeld was talking about his struggles during his early years doing stand-up comedy—including how  he was removed from the sitcom *Benson*. Seinfeld mentioned that he was in his mid-thirties before he finally sold the *Seinfeld* show, and the sale only happened after he had spent more than a dozen years kicking around comedy clubs. Seinfeld said that many actors were older than people thought they were because it took them so long to finally "make it." If you study most actors' biographies, you will usually find a litany of unremarkable jobs that preceded their success. Before getting their breaks, Brad Pitt used to dress up in a chicken suit in front of a fast food restaurant, Ellen DeGeneres was an oyster shucker, and Madonna worked behind a doughnut counter.

Recently, a friend at DreamWorks told me that several applicants she interviewed asked how long it would take for them to become a vice president. It was obvious the applicants had not done any homework on the company, or they would have known that there are no vice presidents at DreamWorks. These applicants also seemed to have the notion that the path to the top was easily attained. It was a matter of "when" they would be vice presidents, not "if." The biggest rewards have to be earned over time. Without the maturity to put off short-term rewards for long-term fulfillment, these prospective employees will have virtually no chance of reaching their ultimate goals. Either they will quickly drop out of the business when they see the commitment that is required, or they will be in for some large disappointment. The key to reaching the highest levels of accomplishment is the ability to put in the hours today for the payoff tomorrow.

INTERVIEW TIPS

Job interviews are a great time to impress a future employer with your drive and ingenuity. I know that looking for a new job can be stressful. Whenever I found  myself job hunting, I was always searching for whatever edge I could find. Every line of business has companies with distinct points of view, and not every person will fit in with every company. Doing research and finding out the "tone" of a company is essential before applying for employment. This background research will improve your employment interview, and you will discover whether that company is the place for you.

The conventional school of thought is that when you interview for a job, you should have some short, thoughtful answers prepared as well as a few questions of your own. I suspect that the advice is effective, but it isn't always the best strategy. When you are interviewing with the person who will be making the final choice, you may want to take a different approach.

A couple of years into my employment at Filmation, Kay Wright told me about an animator/director who was branching out and starting his own studio. The individual was recruiting and Wright felt that I might be a good fit in his start-up company. I knew him from Filmation, but my contact had been limited. The interview would be a chance for the director to find out more about me. After exchanging pleasantries, the interview began, and what followed was surprising. I was anticipating a series of probing questions such as, "Why do you think you would be good at this company?" Instead, what I received was a monologue from the man. He spoke nonstop, describing in detail the plans for his new studio. I listened attentively, nodding in agreement and replying with an occasional "Uh-huh."

After almost an hour, he was interrupted by a phone call and our meeting came to an end. I left the building feeling as if I had bombed the interview; I had not only failed to leave an impression on my potential employer, I seemed invisible. As I drove back to the studio, I was dreading what I would tell Wright. He had graciously arranged this great opportunity, and I had squandered it. When I reached his office, Wright turned to me and said he had just gotten off the phone with the animator/director. I was sick to my stomach.

"He loved you!" Wright informed me. "He's all excited about having you at his company!" I was dumbfounded. How on earth could he be excited about having me work for him? I did not tell him anything about myself. Then it hit me. The interview was not about *me*, it was about *him*. The animator/director was an "alpha leader," a highly-driven, successful talent—with a big ego. As I was sitting there listening to him, the animator/director was projecting all the great feelings he was having about his studio onto me. The less I said, the more he talked. And the more he talked, the smarter, more creative, and more valuable I became.

That interview taught me a great lesson. Whenever I want to make a favorable impression on a highly successful person, I try to turn the focus of the meeting on him or her. I try to get people like that to talk as much as possible about themselves and their ideas. Everyone's favorite subject is him/herself, and when you are dealing with the highest-level achievers, this is especially true.

THINK ON YOUR FEET

Damon Ross, a development executive at DreamWorks, told me how his career was almost snuffed out before it began. When Ross was studying at Vassar College, he knew he wanted to be involved with the movie industry, so he sent out letters to entertainment companies inquiring about potential opportunities. His persistence landed him the chance to interview at the Viacom offices in New York.

As a prospective employee, Ross took a battery of office skill tests at Viacom, and at the end of the session he was informed that the company would be interested in hiring him when he completed college. When he graduated a few months later, Ross moved to New York, rented an apartment, and returned to the Viacom office to lay claim to his outstanding offer. But there was a hitch: the manager who had earlier given Ross the tests was no longer employed by the company—and worse still, there was no record of his application or test results. In an instant, Ross's surefire job offer had vanished.

Ross remembered a letter he had received weeks earlier from an executive at VH-1, one of the cable channels owned by Viacom. Since the VH-1 offices were in the same building as Viacom, Ross took a chance and went to see the executive, who turned out to be exceedingly gracious. The executive didn't have any job openings available, but he did have a friend who had just been promoted to director of development for the newly created movie division of Nickelodeon (also a subsidiary of Viacom), who was looking for an assistant. In just a few moments, Ross was connected with the Nickelodeon executive, whereupon he secured a firm job offer. Ross was successful in his new job, was promoted, and ended up staying with Nickelodeon for twelve years. By thinking on his feet, Ross was able to turn a potentially devastating rejection into a career-making opportunity. "Within twenty minutes I went from 'No' to 'Yes'," he recalled.

LADDER-CLIMBING ADVICE

There are three kinds of workers: those who exceed their job description, those who perform their job description exactly, and those who do less than expected. Guess which

group gets the most promotions? That's right, the ones who do more than they are asked to do. I have gotten into disagreements with people who believe that an employee should never go beyond what he/she is paid for. The people who believe this think if an employee performs beyond his job brief, he is undervaluing his work and not being duly compensated. I disagree with this sort of thinking. I believe that if a person wants to be promoted, then he should act—and perform—at the level of the job he desires. Companies like to know that a job candidate will be successful if he/she is promoted to a new position, and there is no better way to judge job suitability than by seeing that the worker can perform the duties of the job.

Experience has shown me that the usual way to rise up the ladder is to first do the job, and then get paid for it. There is no question that by adopting this approach you may be exploited by an unscrupulous company, but I have never been a victim of such practices. Normally, I have noticed that when a person does perform above his job category, he is rewarded for his service. I would caution, however, that if you find yourself chronically working far beyond your pay grade without a promotion or compensation, you might need to consider looking at another company.

One of the benefits of striving to perform the job you want instead of the job you have is that you allow your employer to visualize you in the new role before you have the position. If you are already operating at a higher level satisfactorily, the company will have greater confidence in promoting you to the new position. I believe that if a worker is only doing the job that he is being paid for, he is probably overpaid. I like to see my colleagues stretching their abilities and assuming new responsibilities. In my opinion everyone gains when a worker performs beyond his/her expectations. The employee benefits by keeping the job interesting while developing his skill set. And the company is rewarded with an individual who is delivering added value. My advice to every employee is to beat expectations. You will not only safeguard yourself from layoffs in future, but you will also be on the path to future promotions.

DRESS FOR THE JOB YOU WANT, NOT THE ONE YOU HAVE

My mother used to stress the importance of dressing right, and I confess to only following her advice intermittently. The fact is, she was right. By coming to work appropriately dressed, you show respect for your position. While this  rule is less ironclad in the creative sphere of the film world, I would urge anyone who wants to work in a more formal business environment to adopt the practice of dressing well. The way we are perceived has a great influence on our future prospects, and dressing suitably for the work environment can be a big boost. (Warning: I caution anyone about excessively over-dressing for your workplace—doing so looks like one-upmanship and can be counterproductive.)

I have worked with dozens of film editors, and Edie Ichioka-Bleiman is right at the top of the list. Edie trained under Walter Murch, who is the godfather of editors (both figuratively and literally—he won Oscars for *The Godfather* and *The Godfather II*), and she is brilliantly talented and insightful. The first thing you will notice about Edie is that she does not dress like other editors. Instead of the commonplace jeans and untucked shirt, Edie wears a well-pressed skirt and blouse. When you step into her editorial suite, her manner of dressing makes an immediate impact. I once asked her why she chose to dress more formally than her peers. She replied that when she first started in the film business she used to dress casually, but decided that she did not want to be seen as the person who lugged around the film cans. She saw herself as one day being an editor, so she presented herself as a potential candidate. She was dressing for the job she wanted, not the one she was in—and her decision paid off.

When the press junkets began for *Bee Movie*, I decided that I would always wear a jacket and tie for the journalists. Although many creatives dress casually, I recalled what Jerry Seinfeld told me he had learned from the more experienced comics when he was starting out on the stand-up circuit: "Always dress better than your audience." Most of his peers would wear casual clothes to their gigs, but Seinfeld wanted to position himself differently. His material was classy and he wanted to project that image. If you find yourself in a position where you need to address an audience, then I suggest you follow the advice that Seinfeld gleaned from those pioneering comedians. Give your audience respect, and they will grant you the same. Each of us has choices to make that will contribute to our success—or serve as potential setbacks. Try to perform at a higher level than expected and present yourself well.

BE KIND TO GATEKEEPERS (BUT TRY TO WORK AROUND THEM)

"Gatekeepers" are those assistants that stand between you and the executives that you want to meet. In case you think the assistants who set the schedules for those people higher up are not significant, then you might want to do a history check on Leon Trotsky. Trotsky, an insider in the Communist Party, was marginalized out of the way by a colleague—the guy who made the appointments to the Politburo. And who was the gatekeeper who set the appointments? Joseph Stalin.

Professor Lee Bobker confided to my NYU film class a trick of the trade. Bobker told us, and rightly so, that those assistants who first answer the phone should become our best friends. He advised us that we would not get anywhere or accomplish anything without their help. The sooner those gatekeepers became your allies, the better off you would be. But, as helpful as these appointment makers might be, sometimes, Bobker cautioned, you would need to circumvent them, and when that happened, he suggested a clever technique.

Bobker proposed that whenever we needed to contact an elusive executive directly, the best time to call would be after 6:00 p.m. His experience was that the office staff would leave on time, but the executive would stay late and thus be more prone to answer his/her phone. I have used Bobker's technique and can vouch that it works. In fact, I call this window of opportunity "the-fences-are-down-at-Jurassic Park" time.

FILM FESTIVALS, CONFERENCES, AND PROFESSIONAL GATHERINGS

If you have ever been to a festival, conference, or expo, you know that the mood is light and the attendees are relaxed. Such conviviality creates the perfect atmosphere for your target to be receptive to your approach. Best of all, there is almost no chance that she will be shielded by her gatekeepers. I have used public gatherings such as these to make contact with people that I would never have had the chance to speak to if I had followed the protocol of calling their offices. Making a first contact at a gathering will put the normal gatekeeper at a huge disadvantage when you later call the executive's office. In your follow-up call, all you have to say is that you spoke with the executive at the fill-in-the-blank gathering, and her assistant will feel compelled to put you through—the gatekeeper won't know at this point how important or inconsequential you are. I used to scan the festival, lecture, and convention listings to locate people that were of interest to me. I can honestly say that every person that I made a first contact with at an event later agreed to read the material I submitted. They might pass on my material, but they always would read what I sent, and that is all that I could ask of them.

7

TRAITS TO AVOID

"Don't walk away from negative people. Run!"
–Stew Leonard, Sr., supermarket owner

One of my favorite comedies is Rob Reiner's *When Harry Met Sally*, a wonderful exposé on the dating rituals between men and women. There is one particular Nora Ephron-scripted exchange between Harry (Billy Crystal) and Sally (Meg Ryan) that strikes me as also being applicable to the work environment. During the scene, Harry speaks of classifying people by how much work they require in a relationship.

```
HARRY: There are two kinds of
    women: high maintenance and low
    maintenance.
SALLY: Which one am I?
HARRY: You're the worst kind; you're
    high maintenance but you think
    you're low maintenance.
```

FOUR WORKER TYPES

In general, workers fall into one of four groups, and I rank their desirability in this order:

- Low Maintenance/High Productivity
- High Maintenance/High Productivity
- Low Maintenance/Low Productivity
- High Maintenance/Low Productivity

Low Maintenance
High Productivity

Just as the label suggests, high-maintenance people require a lot of work. And being classified as an employee who demands excessive attention can affect your career prospects. I was once storyboarding on a project when an experienced artist joined the crew. During the meeting to "launch" this new artist on his assignment, he asked a multitude of questions—or rather, it felt as though the artist were interrogating the director.

High Maintenance
High Productivity

Later the artist mentioned to me that he had just finished his assignment on another one of the studio's projects. He detailed how he had enjoyed storyboarding on the previous movie because the director always spent a great deal of time with him answering his many questions. Having witnessed his cross-examination from the earlier meeting, I had no trouble reading between the lines—the previous director had probably become exhausted from the repeated

Low Maintenance
Low Productivity

High Maintenance
Low Productivity

inquiries and begged his producer to transition this artist off the movie. This artist, although quite good, was a considerable resource drain. Not surprisingly, soon after he joined our project, he once again "finished his assignment." He had crossed the line and had become the dreaded ultra-high-maintenance employee.

Not all high-maintenance employees become drains on their companies. Some very creative artists are high maintenance, but I love working with them because they bring so much to a movie. With these extraordinary talents, the extra effort they require is compensated by their high-quality work. They possess a secondary trait—they also correspondingly fit the category of *high productivity*. An employee who craves attention from his leaders can still fashion a long, successful career if he delivers superior performance. These people fall into the category of High Maintenance/High Productivity.

No employee is less attractive to a manager than one who demands a great deal of attention yet delivers a lackluster performance. Anyone who falls into the High Maintenance/Low Productivity category is just one step from the unemployment line. At the other extreme is the ideal worker, the Low Maintenance/High Productivity person. These achievers provide excellence while requiring little supervision. Any long-term career aspirant should aim to become one of these dynamos. I have been lucky to know such people and I fight to have them on a crew. These colleagues imprint themselves in my memory—and they are the first ones to find work.

Not everyone can be a high-producing engine, but that should not limit your prospects. I know artists who may not be the fastest drawers, but who are undemanding, reliable, and successful in their careers. These people are Low Maintenance/Lower Productivity workers. While they are not the highest achievers, they make up for their shortfalls by being terrific cheerleaders.

All but the High Maintenance/Low Productivity employees can enjoy job longevity. If you find that you are frequently claiming time from your superiors due to your neediness, then you had better be producing more than your coworkers. If you are not, then you are setting yourself up to be replaced. No company in today's competitive landscape can afford a High Maintenance/Low Productivity worker.

DON'T BE TOXIC

When word went out to the artistic community that part of the movie *Who Framed Roger Rabbit?* was going to be animated in Los Angeles, the small unit was deluged with portfolios. Many of the animators in the industry had heard about the exceptional work that was being done in London by Richard Williams's studio, and they were eager to become involved in what was anticipated to be a landmark film. The experience of poring through portfolios is much akin to hunting through garage sales to find that much-coveted piece—sometimes you find gold, but most of the time you leave disappointed. During my years of working in London, I must have reviewed hundreds of portfolios. I learned that I knew whether I was interested in an artist after the first two minutes of viewing his artwork. That may not seem like much time to judge quality, but in fact, great talent leaps at you.

During one of my artist reviews for *Roger Rabbit*, I opened the pages of one black leather binder to reveal exceptional work. The artist's figure drawing work was exceptional—far superior to other submissions. The talent of the person was obvious, and his resume listed a number of well-known films. I was convinced that the owner of this portfolio was an automatic hire.

I was wrong. As soon as I mentioned the name of this artist to the other members of the portfolio review group, I was met with a thundering "NO!" It was as if I had declared that I wanted to introduce the Ebola virus into the primate house. For the next few moments, each of the portfolio reviewers detailed a personal horror story about working with the individual. This particular artist was surly, uncooperative, and, worst of all, destroyed the feeling of camaraderie among the crew.

I couldn't believe that a talent of the magnitude on display before me was unemployable. But that artist was rejected as the group moved onto the next portfolio. I was unaware how destructive one individual employee can be.

Since we never hired that particular difficult artist for *Roger Rabbit*, I was spared an early lesson on how one negative employee can affect a project. But later, when I was in London with Amblimation Studios, I had a front row seat to see how one artist can poison the morale of an entire film. From the beginning of the artist's tenure on the movie, he demonstrated negative behavior—he was consistently late and was modeling bad behavior for the rest of the crew. I was counseled by a top Hollywood producer how to deal with a morale-damaging talent: "It doesn't matter how valuable you think he is to the movie; you have to get rid of a toxic person."

That producer was right—those workers are poison to have around. They are so damaging to a work environment that I call this type of person "radioactive," because they leave a half-life of negativity even after they are gone. The leader has to work harder to help the remaining employees "heal" from the toxic person's gossip, cynicism, and bad habits.

I would love to say that I learned how to deal with toxic people after hearing the producer's quick remedy—after all, the directive could not have been stated more clearly: Get rid of him! However, when I later found myself in a similar situation, I foolishly believed that I could turn around a toxic person's attitude. At the time when I encountered this second toxic person's particular brand of negativity, the production was in need of great talents, and this artist was one of the best. Instead of pulling the trigger and getting rid of the person, I invested more time and energy to see if, by giving him more attention, I could change his behavior. But like a black hole in space, any energy you pour into one of these toxic people is just sucked up without effect. This type of person seems to be unlimited in the amount of negativity he/

she produces, and that is why the top producer was so emphatic about expeditiously severing ties with him/her. As a lucky happenstance, I was saved more extensive damage to the production from this artist because another job opportunity arose and the toxic guy jumped to the new project. (I should mention that toxic people are often opportunistic, and are always on the prowl for the "next great thing.") Because the radioactive artist moved on, the damage left behind was repaired and we ended up taking only a small hit in terms of productivity.

NEVER LET A WORK ISSUE BECOME A PERSONAL ONE

There are problems in the workplace every day; some offer easy solutions while others require adept handling to be resolved. A problematic situation escalates when an employee allows a work issue to turn into a personal issue. When a work issue becomes personal—and the usual reason is ego—the inevitable resolution is the removal of the employee.

I was once working on a project when the studio decided to increase its slate of productions. The anticipated increase of movies required the studio to add another person to oversee the films. As soon as the new executive joined the company, one of the members of our group chafed at the changed work dynamic. Before the new supervisor arrived, our team had enjoyed relative autonomy for our project—although, admittedly, we had spent too much money. And now, there were more restrictions on how we would operate. The studio had been patient with us, but they felt our inexperience was showing and we needed oversight from a seasoned professional. Unfortunately, instead of viewing this recruit as a resource, my colleague viewed him as a threat and made no secret of his disapproval. Everyone who came into contact with this disgruntled coworker was told tales of how horrible the new supervisor was, and the situation was becoming very uncomfortable.

At first, the team members joked about our "elephant in the room" gatherings, but soon the escalating animus between the pair was impacting production. Suddenly, the problems of the movie could not be addressed in meetings because of the tangible tension between the two. What had started as a work problem (the need for some studio oversight) had become a personal problem. And specifically, a personal problem that pointed at the contentious member of our team. Numerous conversations took place in an attempt to massage the relationship between the crewmember and the new studio executive, and all were unsuccessful. Finally, the only viable course of action for the studio was to reassign the worker. The employee was a valuable member of the studio, and the hope was that by moving the employee into another role, the situation would work out. As might have been expected, the crewmember never adjusted to the new studio structure and eventually left. But the situation never needed to escalate to the nuclear scenario of an "either he leaves or I leave" ultimatum.

When a work problem turns into one of a personal nature, then the usual outcome is that the employee is removed (i.e., terminated). Let me put it bluntly: when it becomes apparent that *you are the problem, then getting rid of you becomes the solution.* No company can afford to allow its business to be hijacked by an employee who turns what should be a work issue into a personal problem. The crewmember I mentioned above committed the ultimate sin when he allowed his personal feelings to escalate into an untenable business situation. When an employee draws a line in the sand stating that he cannot work with another person, then he is signing his own death warrant.

DON'T VENT IMMEDIATELY. WAIT A DAY, AND SEE IF YOU FEEL THE SAME WAY.

All of us have egos, and sometimes things happen at our workplaces that cause us to react with displeasure. When confronted by those situations, our first thought is to wish to set the record straight or voice our irritation. My best advice to you is: don't! Do not race to the person and unload your wrath in the passion of the moment. (As a note, let me say that I am talking about routine professional situations, not grossly out of line instances such as sexual harassment or outright bigotry. Those affronts must be addressed immediately.) Anger—much like the negativity that is left over from toxic employees—has a half-life. When anger is released, there is always some residual resentment. Just because you feel better after you have unloaded your displeasure does not mean the recipient of your outburst recovers as quickly. The residue of the anger can linger and create a strained working relationship.

When I was working on *The Prince of Egypt*, there was a day when I let my ego get the best of me. I went to the producer's office to vent my frustrations, but she was not available, so I had to wait until the next day to see her. In the ensuing hours, my bruised ego healed and I realized that my complaint was trivial. That day was many years ago, and I have no memory of why I was so worked up, but I am still glad that I did not embarrass myself. By waiting until the next day to see the producer, I gave my anger time to dissipate. Had I managed to meet with the producer immediately, the problem would have escalated, and I am certain I would have regretted my actions once I had cooled off the next day.

Backing off for a day to judge the scope of a problem is a win-win scenario. If the individual feels the same way when she returns to work a day later, then she should bring up the issue. If, however, the person realizes that her emotions took hold of her, then she is spared the awkwardness of having to recover from some misplaced words. I have seen several outbursts over the years, and usually the person is forgiven, but occasionally the eruption can leave a lingering scar on the person's reputation.

In a creative environment, the likelihood of crossing egos rises, and flare-ups are common. When you work with passionate, committed individuals, defending turf and ideas is part of the process, and sometimes people will get so wrapped up in their convictions that they react too strongly. By waiting the extra day before addressing your concern, you allow yourself the chance to determine if your problem is really about the work, or whether you are responding to a bruised ego. An additional advantage to waiting before bringing up your issue is that you give yourself extra time to compose your thoughts. A well-organized and objective argument will give you a far greater chance of success than storming into a room with a collection of perceived affronts.

Prevent yourself from exacerbating problems by stepping back from the issue at hand and permitting yourself a cooling-off period. I can promise that you will never regret having waited an extra day before addressing a contentious issue, and you may save yourself some time-consuming reputation control. James Dent, the humorist and political cartoonist, said something I try to remember whenever I feel my ego starting to emerge. He said, "As you go through life you are going to have many opportunities to keep your mouth shut. Take advantage of all of them."

AT LEAST NOBODY HAS TO FOLLOW YOU WITH ANTI-VENOM

During a vacation in Costa Rica, I visited a banana plantation. On the tour, the guide explained that when the workers head out each morning to pick bananas, there is always one person assigned to carry the basket with the snake anti-venom. Occasionally a worker would startle a poisonous snake. Since the snake's poison is so fast acting, it was important for the workers to carry anti-venom with them into the banana fields—otherwise, they might lose a worker.

As we continued the tour, I thought about the banana workers in a new light. These guys were the ones with hard jobs. No matter how difficult I might think my job is some days, it is nothing in comparison to these men and women. After all, even on my very, very worst day of work, I do not require someone walking alongside me carrying a syringe of anti-venom to save my life.

Putting our work complaints into perspective can make our problems seem less significant. Whatever our perceived job difficulties may be, there are those in worse situations. Instead of focusing on the disparities between yourself and your colleagues, take inventory of the things that you could do better and put your energies into fixing them. The real fact of the matter is that none of us do our jobs identically—even if we are doing essentially the same job.

8

IMPROVE YOUR SKILLS

"It is not the strongest or the most intelligent who will survive
but those who can best manage change."
—Charles Darwin

1982 was a pivotal year for the animation industry. Studios were increasingly sending work overseas, and the pool of jobs was shrinking daily. The entertainment field has always been volatile and cyclical, but in 1982 the state of animation seemed precarious even to veteran cartoonists. It was within this unfortunate perfect storm of unemployment, outsourcing, and a changing business model that the contract covering the animation artists expired. I had been working in the animation field for barely three years when the union called a strike.

Labor disputes are invariably unpleasant situations. They create animosity on both sides, and usually after a prolonged work stoppage, an agreement is reached. Nobody really wins in a strike, and the cartoonists' strike of 1982 was typical in that regard. The studios managed to retain the rights to send work offshore, but they made concessions to raising hourly minimums and adding holidays. Although my tenure in the industry had been short when the strike hit, finding only ten weeks of work in all of 1982 imprinted a lesson on me that I have carried ever since:

> "When the bad times come, the top sliver of talent still manages to find work."

During that long period without work, I continued to knock on doors and, while moving from studio to studio, studied what type of person was still employed. I discovered that these Darwinian survivors all had one common denominator: they were the best in the field and they could perform a variety of functions. These were top talents, but also utility artists of the highest order.

Since I had only three years of the lowest level experience, I was running at the back of the herd. I finally got the message loud and clear: if I did not improve my skills and widen my breadth of knowledge, I was going to be vulnerable to every downturn. I felt like the worst, out-of-shape walk-on at a college football tryout.

The only chance I would have to make the team would be if they expanded the roster.

As luck would have it, that is what happened.

The animation business was about to undertake a profound shift. A new business model was emerging—the behemoth of syndicated television. At the beginning of 1983, Filmation Studios landed an order for a then-unheard-of sixty-five episodes of what would become the TV animation sensation, *He-Man and the Masters of the Universe*. During the 1982 strike, Filmation was the only major TV animation studio in Los Angeles to refuse to send work overseas. To his credit, Lou Scheimer, the studio's head, kept hundreds of jobs in town, and, in 1983, one of those jobs was mine. Even though I landed a plum assignment as a storyboard artist, I was aware that my skill set was in need of improvement. I had just limped through a disaster of a year, and I knew that if I wanted to avoid being in a similar position in the future, I had better improve my skills. To do that, I had to get some expert, classical training. And in 1983, there was only one place to go—Walt Disney Studios.

Instead of being overwhelmed by the prospect of trying to get hired by a studio that had rejected me four years earlier, I put together a focused game plan. Fortunately for me, Glenn Vilppu, one of Disney's top layout artists, was teaching drawing classes at a local school. I knew that my best chance to learn the Disney style of drawing was to learn from a master like Vilppu. In order to take the drawing class, I had to sacrifice some luxuries, as the cost of the art lessons exceeded my weekly salary. By the second week of class, however, I realized that taking one drawing class a week was not going to be sufficient. My skills were rudimentary, and if I wanted to apply to Disney the following year, I was going to need more practice. Since I could not afford a second class with Vilppu, I signed up for a life drawing class at a local community college. The teacher, Martin Mondrus, was excellent. He taught a different approach to life drawing, and the two classes complemented each other. My work began to improve with two art classes a week. I knew that a hallmark of the Disney style was its anthropomorphic animals, and the review board would want to see animal drawings and quick action sketches in my portfolio. I expanded my learning approach to include a drawing session at the zoo every Saturday and a few hours sketching at the park on Sundays. Before I was aware of it, I had baby-stepped my way to a four-day-a-week educational process.

For the next year, I continued my artist's boot camp. Especially advantageous was the fact that my job as a storyboard artist on *He-Man* gave me the daily opportunity to apply what I was learning. I could feel my artistic muscles growing, and in March 1984, after fifteen months of studying, I was ready to apply to Disney Studios. I was lucky to have a friend, Larry White, working at Disney, and he helped me organize my portfolio. I found White's critical eye invaluable, and when I was eventually accepted at Disney, I knew I owed a large part of my success to his advice.

During my hiring interview, Don Hahn, a talented producer who later became another in a succession of mentors, laid out the parameters of the job. The studio was in the process of finishing *The Black Cauldron* and they could only guarantee me nine months of employment as a trainee in-betweener at an entry-level salary. At the time, I was working as an assistant storyboard supervisor, and the Disney offer represented a pay cut of almost fifty percent. Clearly, the terms were not exactly what I was hoping for, but I was not looking to join Disney for the money. I wanted an education and that was worth what I hoped would be a temporary pay cut. What I was more concerned about, however, was the idea that I might be out of work again before Christmas.

I told Hahn, "I know you are only promising me work until the end of the year, but I plan to work so hard, be so productive, and be so cheap, that in nine months time, you won't be able to afford to lay me off." At the time, I think Hahn may have been amused by my words, but whatever the case, on March 19, 1984, I walked onto the Disney lot for the first time as an employee.

Nine months later, when *The Black Cauldron* ended, just as I had predicted, Disney kept me on—even as they laid off other artists. In the preceding months, I had worked almost every weekend and volunteered for every odd job possible.

EVERY SKILL IS IMPORTANT. THE ONE YOU LEARN TODAY MAY SAVE YOU TOMORROW.

When I joined Disney, the common practice was for the most junior person on an animator's team to shoot the video pencil tests. Since the studio was filled with artists who loved to draw, no one wanted to be reduced to  sitting in a dark room and shooting the animation tests on the video machine. One Friday afternoon, Don Hahn mentioned that the film had a backlog of animation scenes that needed to be shot for approval. More importantly, he was worried that they would miss their week's quota if the animation was not shot in time to be shown to the movie's directors. I told Hahn that I was intimately familiar with the testing machines. My first job in the animation business had been shooting animation pencil tests for Filmation Studios, and to Hahn's delight, I volunteered to come in on Saturday and clear the backlog.

Since the Disney animation staff was working overtime, the amount of animation to be shot was much larger than usual. But I was used to working with a staff of seventy-five to one hundred animators at Filmation—as opposed to about twenty-five at Disney—so I had no trouble completing the task. By early afternoon, I had finished shooting the tests for the directors' approval, and we stayed on schedule. After that Saturday, I became the "go to" guy for pencil tests and, most significantly, I had positioned myself as being indispensable. Later, when *The Black Cauldron* was completed, Disney was forced to downscale their crew because the next movie, *The Great Mouse Detective*, was not planned to be as ambitious. I was kept on at the studio even as others were given their layoff notices. I would never have guessed that my months of shooting pencil tests in a closet at Filmation would be the skill that I needed at Disney.

At the age of twenty-seven, I had successfully made the transition into feature film animation at the best-known company in the world. Most importantly, however, I was taking steps toward entering the top echelon in the field of animation, in order to vaccinate myself against the inevitable downturns in the business. When the next animation slump occurred in late 1987, I proved myself valuable to Don Hahn, and when he needed someone to work with him at Disney's London unit on *Who Framed Roger Rabbit?,* I was chosen.

BE YOUR OWN SCULPTOR

Since the 1982 strike, the animation business has experienced many cycles of boom and bust, but I have been lucky to remain employed during those lean periods. I have weathered those bad times because I took inventory of my weaknesses early in my career and implemented steps to overcome them. I now refer to those painful months as my "Year of Living Precariously." My lesson was well learned. The higher my skill level, the more valuable I was in the workplace. My inspiration for examining my own shortcomings came from a person I had never met: Arnold Schwarzenegger.

When I was in college, I first learned of the future actor/governor when my teacher, Larry Silk, screened a movie he had edited: George Butler's watershed bodybuilding documentary, *Pumping Iron*. In the film, Schwarzenegger speaks of how, as a bodybuilder, he analyzes his body just as a sculptor would a work of art. Schwarzenegger says that when he finds a particular muscle mass of his that is lacking in some way, he exercises that body part until he achieves the symmetry and perfection he requires. The idea of taking inventory of personal weaknesses and then disciplining yourself to correct them impressed me.

I applied Schwarzenegger's method to fine-tuning my artistic skills. I have since learned that improving oneself is an ongoing process, and I am always examining the field of animation in an attempt to anticipate where it will be heading. I think about what new skills will be required, and I take steps to master those skills. Viewing yourself as your own personal sculptor is intelligent counsel and I urge everyone to take up this productive habit. Periodically, take personal inventory and decide where you can be better. Once you have identified those areas, make them your personal projects.

Many companies have employee reviews that codify this process. But even if your place of employment has such a process, do not wait for your next review to begin. Start today and you will thank yourself. Become your own project—turn today's weaknesses into tomorrow's strengths. You will become imminently more employable, and you will have more fun at work as well.

IF YOU CAN'T SOLVE A PROBLEM IN A REASONABLE AMOUNT OF TIME, FIND SOMEONE WHO CAN

During my early days on *The Black Cauldron*, I would on occasion come across a position for a character that was difficult for me to draw. No matter how

hard I struggled to solve the drawing, I could not get the character to have the required appeal and look. Fortunately for me, my roommate happened to be the assistant animator for Andreas Deja—the artist who had designed the characters for the film. So, when Deja stopped by to check the work of my office mate, I asked him if he might also help me with my drawing. While it is true that continually having people solve problems for you might create a dependency, this was not the case with my question for Deja. While he was working through my drawing problem, I was watching the way he worked. I did not ask him to coach me through the entire process, and instead focused my query on one particular sticking point. By studying his demonstration, I was learning the correct way to draw the character, and once I had seen the way he worked, I could successfully draw the character myself.

On that day, I learned the value of not allowing myself to become paralyzed over a small detail in a large task—especially when there was an expert available who could solve the problem. I realized I was preventing a huge scene in the movie from being finished because I could not make a tiny part of one drawing look right. To me, the problem seemed insurmountable, but to Deja—who had designed the characters—the solution was easy. Once he showed me how to draw the character from that angle, my worries were over. Since that episode, I have noticed how common it is for some employees to sweat over a problem instead of seeking help from a colleague.

If you were writing a paper about the Battle of Gettysburg, would you stop in the middle of your writing and wrack your brain for an hour trying to recall the exact date the skirmish started, or would you jump over to Google and do a quick search? I would hope that once you realized that you were struggling with some information, you would decide to consult a reference. I suggest you take the approach you use for research and apply that technique to work situations. If you find yourself battling with a difficult problem, give yourself a reasonable amount of time to solve it on your own, and then if you are still wrestling with the issue, seek out someone who has more experience. I have found that the strongest talents are happy to help, often finding your interest in their knowledge flattering.

You can move beyond your immediate coworkers and seek help elsewhere if necessary. When I am working on a film with the writers or storyboard artists and we run into a story difficulty, I find it useful to think of a similar type of movie that I enjoy. By studying how another writer or director has solved an equivalent problem, I can generate ideas that will resolve our issue.

IF YOU WANT TO CREATE CAREER LONGEVITY, YOU MUST REINVENT YOURSELF EVERY FIVE YEARS

Since *Bee Movie* was released, Jerry Seinfeld has created both a reality TV show *(The Marriage Ref)* and an Internet show *(Comedians in Cars Getting Coffee)*, directed a Broadway show (Colin Quinn in *Long Story Short)*, guest hosted a morning TV program, collaborated with a rap artist, and written and starred in commercials. And that is from the guy who created one of the greatest comedy shows in TV history and has thirty years of stand-up comedy experience. Let me be blunt: if you are performing your job in the same manner five years from now, you are placing yourself at the top of your occupation's endangered species list. Over the past thirty-plus years I have spent in animation, I have watched the animation industry shrink significantly as new techniques and advances wiped out jobs that had previously stood for decades. The only way to combat redundancy in the years ahead is to continually reinvent the way you work.

DON'T BE LAST YEAR'S FASHION AT THIS YEAR'S PRICES

Have you ever been to an after-Christmas sale? If so, then you recall the rows of clothes with marked-down prices, all reduced to make way for the new spring fashions. Job skills are not quite

as volatile as fashion, but they can just as easily become obsolete. New, talented employees are continually entering the workforce—workers who are hungry for success and are armed with the latest skills and knowledge. When we fail to keep pace with what's new in our field, we risk being tossed aside like one of those garments on the sale tables. I am well aware of how quickly fashions change in the movie business. New talent is always on the horizon and one of my self-motivational mantras is: "Remember that there is some twenty-one-year-old graduate out there who is waiting to take my job—and is willing to work harder for less money."

I find the influx of new talent stimulating and exciting. Just as an aquarium needs to have its water cycled, a workplace that experiences a constant change in people who are brimming with enthusiasm and new ideas will be refreshed. Over the years, I have enjoyed watching animation transition from being largely the domain of white males to becoming more diverse. With such diversity, the environment has become more interesting, and we are striving to make our stories more ambitious. The influx of new talent should forever be a reminder that we need to keep our job skills current. For an established professional, experience is a valuable asset—but only if that seasoned knowledge is for a skill that is in demand. Stay in fashion and you will stay employed.

PART II

LEADING and GROWING

q

MOVING INTO MANAGEMENT

"The greater the obstacle, the more glory in overcoming it."
—Molière

I have noticed that a newly appointed supervisor's transition to a leadership position is often awkward. The newly minted leader needs to understand that, unlike in his previous role, where his success was based upon his own achievements, the manager's success is dependent upon the result that his team produces. In my years in animation, I have seen great artists promoted to department supervisors who have then struggled with this dynamic.

These first-time supervisors also discover that they are now responsible for giving out assignments, and consequently their ability to plan becomes critical. When I was working at Amblimation in London, I became aware of how ill-prepared many of our freshly promoted managers were. In fact, I was the guiltiest of all. Although I had held some production management jobs, none of them prepared me for the magnitude of responsibilities that I assumed when I became the associate producer on *An American Tail II: Fievel Goes West.*

The first *American Tail* movie had been produced by Don Bluth and his crew, but in the years since its release, he had moved his company to Dublin and was in production on a series of his own projects. With Bluth and his talented team no longer available, Amblin decided to build their own animation studio in London from the ground up. And with Amblimation being such a new studio, there was a void in terms of managerial experience; almost all of us were rookies in our new positions. Every day on the film turned out to be such a ride for me on the learning curve, and I sought out any management book that I could get my hands on. I realized that although I had spent a decade working in the animation field, virtually all of my experience was as an artist, and almost none of my background was in managing a big group of people.

I could also see that the journey of self-discovery that I was undergoing was not unique. Every newly promoted department head on the movie was struggling. Although our new department managers may have spent years training to be at the top of their artistic disciplines, they were expected to step into a role as a leader without any training whatsoever. No wonder so many of them (myself included) were floundering. No reasonable leader would expect a person to grab a brush and paint a magnificent landscape without any previous experience, and yet here we were asking our best artists to become managers without the slightest instruction. Promoting people without any training is absurd, but that same mistake is repeated in company after company.

MANAGERS AND LEADERS

In the past few paragraphs I have used the words "manager" and "leader" interchangeably, in the hopes that you would associate them as one type of person. Now, I want you to think about

some of the subtle differences between managers and leaders. I have worked with a lot of wonderful people who I felt were great managers, but I would not classify them as leaders. The roles of managers and leaders are different and require separate skills. Managers control resources, and that usually means people, equipment, and money. Leaders, on the other hand, *guide* and *lift up* the employees. They have the ability to focus people on a task and imbue the job with a higher sense of purpose. Leaders do not arise from some select pool of talent. Leaders can come from every corner of a company, and, in fact, often do. Under the right circumstances, the skills that allow a person to become a leader emerge and that person takes charge.

There is no one leadership profile; every person in charge finds his own way of heading a group. Nick Park, the genius behind the Academy Award-winning films featuring the characters Wallace and Gromit, is a fabulous leader. He is also extremely soft-spoken and exceptionally polite. He is masterful at leading a film crew of dozens of artists while retaining his singular vision, as evidenced by the bookshelves full of awards he has won and the universal affection held for him by his peer group. His leadership style is influenced by his broad artistic skill set—he writes, designs, and gives precise direction on how the characters should act. Although he may be the director, he makes every person feel that he/she is a co-author, and his crews adore working with him.

FIND YOUR FIT

One of the most diabolical creations from the garment industry is the item that reads, "One size fits all." Whenever I read that label on a purchase, I know that I will be wearing something uncomfortable. All of us are built differently, yet somehow the creator of the "one size fits all" object believes his/her article will magically defy logic and fulfill all our needs. My experience tells me that there are few things that will work for everyone. In the same vein, I fully appreciate that not every principle I have included in this book will be a perfect fit for every occupation and for where you are in your life's journey. The key to reading this book is to adopt the ideas that fit your job, your life, and your goals.

Finding work that best suits us requires some experimentation. Not every project is right for every artist. There have been countless times where I have seen an artist struggle on one project, only to move to another movie and excel. The problem with the first assignment was not that the artist was unskilled, but rather, that the film did not fit with the person's sensibilities. There are variables with every job; the duties required, the work atmosphere, the attitude of coworkers, and other differences affect our "fit" with the company. Sometimes a company will be well suited to one person, while another individual will chafe in the same environment.

In the early eighties, the animation department at Disney had under its umbrella two of the most iconic and successful artists imaginable, John Lasseter and Tim Burton. Both Lasseter and Burton possess tremendous talent, but their unique abilities were not a good fit for the regimentation of the assistant animation pool at the studio. In the case of John Lasseter, his interests drew him to the world of computer animation. Once he found his niche at Pixar Animation, he became the "Walt Disney" of the digital era.

Tim Burton's quirky, delightful design sense was not a good match for Disney's classically animated film, *The Black Cauldron*, but his style was magical in *Alice in Wonderland*, *Pee Wee's Big Adventure*, *Beetlejuice*, and the *Batman* movies. The men realized that their true calling lay outside of the world of classical animation that they had trained for at the California Institute of the Arts, and they were perceptive enough to follow their true passions.

The leadership at the Disney Studios did recognize the talents of Lasseter and Burton, even though the two artists ultimately moved in other directions. At Disney, I once saw Tim Burton's inspirational artwork for a movie called *Trick or Treat*, as well as a model sheet of dragons that he had designed for *The Black Cauldron*. John Lasseter was given the task of creating a test for *Where the Wild Things Are* utilizing a computerized camera, to which Glen Keane later added traditional hand-drawn animation. The studio knew that Lasseter and Burton had special talents, but the department was not able at that time to take advantage of them. Neither Burton's *Trick or Treat* endeavor nor Lasseter's *Where the Wild Things Are* project came to fruition, but both artists have since returned to work with Disney.

MAKING AN IMPACT

When I was producing, I would often have artists ask what they could do to be promoted so they could make more money. They would see artists of seemingly equal talent and productivity working at the studio, and one would be promoted while the other one stayed at the same level. To me, the difference between the artists was significant, and the reason why one was being paid more was elementary: the better-paid artist made a far greater impact on the movie than the other artist. I found that there were two kinds of artists: those who understood how to make their work impact the big picture, and those who would focus their energy only on what was before them.

The two types of artists may have looked the same to the other crewmembers, but they were profoundly different. Although both artists might create an equal number of drawings each week, one of the artists would have a far-reaching effect on an entire sequence in the movie while the other would only have an impact on one shot.

Imagine two bricklayers, both of whom set down one thousand bricks at the end of a week. One of the bricklayers sets the cornerstones for five buildings with his bricks, while the other one uses his one thousand bricks to create a small portion of one wall. Which one is worth more to you? Although they may both lay one thousand bricks, they are not workers of equal value to the company. One of them has vision and thinks in terms of the big picture, while the other worker's thinking is confined to a small sphere of influence. The "cornerstone bricklayer" thinks in successively larger terms: this brick goes in this wall, which goes in this structure, which is a part of an entire building project.

The thought process of maximizing the impact of your work is what distinguishes the potential supervisory employee from his colleagues.

10

COMMUNICATION: THE FOUNDATION FOR SUCCESS

"Communication – the human connection – is the key to personal and career success."

– Paul J. Meyer, businessman

In the brilliant movie *Cool Hand Luke*, Paul Newman plays the title character, a convict who is forced to work on a road gang under the prison's captain, a cruel martinet played by Strother Martin. During one of the captain's excessive reprimands, he utters one of cinema's most famous lines, "What we've got here is failure to communicate." We can be thankful that none of us will likely work under such oppressive circumstances, but I am almost certain that each of us has suffered from communication failures. I have worked in England, Canada, and the United States on over a dozen feature films, several television shows, and a couple of television specials, and on almost every production, no matter where it was being made, or where in the hierarchy I was, I have heard the crew lament the lack of communication. And in some of those cases, I was the guilty party responsible for not disseminating important information.

BE VISIBLE

Having had only the slightest command of managerial skills, I was delighted when I stumbled across Tom Peters's book, *In Search of Excellence*, as I was trying to wrangle a television special for Dis-ney back in 1986. While reading Peters's book, I had a major realization as I learned about what the author calls MBWA or "Managing by Walking Around." Peters suggests—or rather, implores—that managers get out of their offices and make face-to-face contact with workers on a regular basis. With the advent of e-mail, instant messaging, and cell phones, the temptation to avoid actual floor time is greater than ever. There is no question that e-mailing or calling a coworker on the phone is a more efficient manner in which to pass on information, but none of the technological alternatives have the same wallop as enabling your employees to see you in their workspace.

I am amazed at how often Jeffrey Katzenberg makes appearances at studio events and even goes from room to room to connect with the crewmembers on a film. Here is a man who is running a huge entertainment company dealing with amusement parks, animated movies, television, theater productions, merchandising, and a huge China initiative, and yet he finds the time to make sure he is connecting with his employees on a personal level. Katzenberg knows that his presence is what makes DreamWorks different from all the other entertainment companies. At every other studio in town, the everyday employee sights the bosses about as often as he sees Bigfoot. But a DreamWorks employee knows that Katzenberg will personally call or a pay a visit to him/her when he/she celebrates an important company anniversary. And this is part of the reason DreamWorks Animation is the only entertainment company listed on the *Fortune* 100 Best Companies to Work For. Katzenberg's commitment to stay in touch with the crew is inspiring, and has made me question myself when I do not get out on the floor enough. "If Jeffrey can do it with all the things he is involved with, then why can't I?" The answer of course is obvious. Any one of us can stay in contact with our crew—if we make being available to others our priority.

When I was working in London for Amblimation Studios, there was nothing more exciting than the days when Steven Spielberg would go on rounds by the artists' desks to look at their work. There is tremendous excitement generated when a celebrity such as Spielberg enters the room. When I was working on *Bee Movie* with Jerry Seinfeld, even though the crew was working with him nearly every day, Seinfeld's presence in the meetings brought about a fresh burst of excitement and creativity. Somehow, just being with either Spielberg or Seinfeld made everyone want to be the best.

You are probably thinking, "Of course people want to do their best work around Spielberg or Seinfeld; they're celebrities." True, but it also works for other leaders. When the leader of a project interacts with the crew, it shows that he/she cares about the people

and the product—and when the leaders show that they care, they get others to invest in the ideas.

A friend told me of a former boss who did not allow the employees to speak to him. If one of his workers needed to contact him, she had to e-mail him, and he would respond when time permitted. When I heard this story, I figured he must have seen *The Wizard of Oz* one too many times—except this guy was hiding behind a cyber-curtain. I cannot imagine a person creating a worse climate for the people in his department. Talk about being disenfranchised—the poor people working under that misanthrope were reminded on an hourly basis just how unimportant they were. When this boss was finally fired, one of the people in the department walked into the break room to find her coworkers discussing the news. Unaware of the situation, she remarked, "It seems like there is a party going on here."

Communicating to those who report to you is only half of the equation; a new leader also needs to recognize her other duty—communicating with the higher-ups in the organization.

Stepping into the role of a supervisor seldom comes with an instruction book, and no one was more aware of this fact than I was. I made every error possible during my early days as a producer. Perhaps my most grievous misstep was trying to solve production problems myself and not involving the studio executives earlier. I mistakenly believed that my task as a leader was to fix every complication on my own and not bother my superiors, but that was exactly the wrong way to operate. Communicating should not be confined to a dialogue with those who work under you. When you move into a managerial or supervisory position, you need to recognize that an important part of your new duties will be keeping your superiors informed. Successful managers and supervisors with the strongest career trajectory are always updating their leaders.

Those executives above you are there to help you, and by communicating with them on a constant basis and informing them of any troubles on the horizon, you are not showing weakness, but instead are displaying excellent managerial skills. Make sure your superiors know what you are doing and keep them abreast of your team's progress. Most importantly, bring up any problem areas as soon as you become aware of them. The longer a supervisor waits to address a difficult issue, the greater the chance that there will be less possible solutions to the issue. It is unlikely that you will be fired for over-communicating with your superiors, but you will be fired if you withhold information and a major problem arises.

GOOD MORALE IS GOOD BUSINESS

I had the great fortune of meeting George Shapiro and Howard West while working on *Bee Movie* with Jerry Seinfeld. Shapiro and West have been Seinfeld's managers for over twenty-five years in an industry where loyalties seem to be an inconvenience. Having witnessed George Shapiro in action for an extended length of time, I cannot imagine anyone who would not want to work with him. There is virtually no one who can make you feel more special and important than Shapiro can. He is a ball of affection, and when he speaks with you, his every inquiry is genuine. Personal management is not just a job title to Shapiro—it is the way he lives his life.

If you think making the effort of ensuring good morale is too expensive for you, then try not having it. I once worked on a movie that suffered from every problem imaginable, starting with a story that never quite came together. While we tried to correct the story issues, the crew valiantly kept working through all the missteps—but the day-to-day morale was lower than any other project on which I have worked. As it became obvious to everyone that the movie was never going to be as good as we had hoped, many people in the crew turned their focus to how much money they were making and whether they could wrangle a promotion. With our goodwill at a low point, the cost of the film spiraled. Because there was little job satisfaction for the artists, their attention turned to their remuneration.

By comparison, the next film had almost an identical crew, but this time the experience turned out to be joyful. The positive morale proved to be beneficial—the film was not only significantly better, but also was produced for a third less money. After having struggled through a painful production with the earlier film, the crew was delighted to be working on a story that was better conceived. The result was an improved environment and a more creative product. When people are having fun at work, productivity goes up and you can save a lot of money. A company cannot have good morale without good communication between the leadership and the employees.

WHEN YOU DELIVER A MESSAGE, IT IS YOUR JOB TO MAKE SURE THE POINT GETS ACROSS

One of the greatest pleasures of working on a movie in London was that the crew was comprised of so many different nationalities. Before I moved to England, I had been working at Disney in Burbank, California where almost all of crewmembers were from the United States. Yes, there were a few foreign nationals—most notably, the renowned animator Andreas Deja from Germany—but the vast amount of the artists were American. Once we began recruiting in London for *An American Tail II*, it became obvious that we would need to widen our talent search and create a multinational crew. In short time, we had artists from Germany, France, Italy, Denmark, Bulgaria, Spain, Brazil, Luxembourg, Finland, Greece, and Turkey, and we used to brag that we were our own microcosm of the United Nations, with over eighteen languages being spoken on the animation floor. Such diversity presented the studio with a terrific opportunity. We found that within our four walls we had the perfect testing spot to see whether a joke or a story point would communicate in the international market. Despite the advantages of having so many nationalities under one roof, I did experience some difficulties. I sometimes found that the crew was misinterpreting the way I was phrasing messages. While an all-American crew would have had little trouble comprehending my idiomatic expressions, our international crew was missing my meaning. During meetings, I would believe that I was carefully laying out the studio policies, and then react with frustration when they were misunderstood. Feeling that I had communicated my expectations perfectly, I would then (wrongly) lay the blame on the artists whenever there was a breach of studio etiquette.

Until I moved to England, my experience in the animation industry had consisted of working in well-established studios like Filmation or Disney where every artist understood the expectation of being on time. Animation has a high degree of interconnectivity between departments and if people are not available when they are supposed to be, the work flow slows down. When Amblimation was started in London, however, there was not an available pool of experienced feature animators, so we had to develop a lot of our own talent. These nascent artists had never worked within the structure of a big studio, and many of them were used to the fluid hours of the television advertising industry. The artists from the commercial world were in the habit of setting their own work schedules and putting in crazy all-nighters to finish their projects on time. While such a process was successful for a ten- or fifteen-second advertisement, the idea of 250 artists keeping such variable hours was unworkable over a two-year time frame. In addition to time-keeping issues, we were experiencing difficulties with the artists' inability to follow our workflow process and expectations.

My first reaction was to blame the artists for the recurring problems, but I began to realize that the fault lay with me, the messenger. Only after my words were repeatedly misunderstood did I accept that it was my responsibility as a communicator to get the information across. I had wrongly believed that the way I had communicated to crewmembers in a Los Angeles studio would translate to this new studio. I found that I had become lazy when instructing crewmembers and had developed shorthand that was incomprehensible to the artists for whom English was a second language. With the burden upon my shoulders, I started to make sure that the recipients understood the instructions that I was giving. I had learned an important message for any leader or manager: take ownership when giving out information. After I began checking to see if my message was received, I found that the compliance rate of the studio policies rose. The foreign nationals were no longer leaving meetings unsure of what was expected, and I had taken a big personal step on the way to becoming a better leader.

TWO HEADS ARE NOT BETTER THAN ONE WHEN THEY WON'T AGREE

I have witnessed movies being made where the two co-directors had opposing ideas—and the result was disastrous. On one particular film, the directors could not agree on something as simple as a character's wardrobe, and so the costume would change from sequence to sequence depending upon which director was supervising. The situation escalated to such a degree—and the crew grew so confused—that the production office literally had to issue a memo to let the artists know which costume the lead character was wearing in each sequence. The most insane part of the whole scenario was that the two directors seemed to enjoy each other's company. They lunched together each day, but they just could not agree on this one point. On another film, I witnessed great animosity between departments with each one blaming the other for mistakes. When the communication and collaboration between departments deteriorates to such a degree, it creates a *Lord of the Flies*-type dynamic within the crew, and success is nearly impossible to achieve. Incidentally, those movies with warring factions disappointed at the box office. Fortunately, most of the projects I have worked on have been blessed with excellent communication between the departments and supervisors who trusted their team members.

HOW YOU SAY IT IS AS IMPORTANT AS WHAT YOU SAY

Have you ever received an e-mail where the sender has typed out the MESSAGE IN ALL CAPITAL LETTERS? What is your reaction? Doesn't it feel as if the sender is screaming at you? Even if the content of the missive is benign, the way the words come across seems aggressive. In general, any words in print appear more severe than they would be if they were spoken. Emoticons were invented to make sure the intentions of the sender of an e-mail were clear, but these cute little figures do not work well in all business settings.

When I was working in London, the time difference between Los Angeles and London forced me to communicate through a lot of faxes. (Today, those faxes would be e-mails.) Frank Marshall, one of the movie's executive producers, was a master of creating the perfect balance between being conversational yet businesslike. His memos captured Marshall's friendly persona, and when I read them, I not only knew what he wanted me to do next, but also that he was aware of the daily difficulties of making a movie. He never, ever used the phrase "A.S.A.P." or "as soon as possible" in any of his memos. This is unusual, considering the high cost of making movies and how pricey missed deadlines can be. (I suspect he figured that, when making movies, everything is imperative. A.S.A.P. is redundant.) Marshall had a real talent for delivering his message in exactly the right way. Whether the news was good or bad, Marshall managed to be caring and empathetic. In every fax, Marshall would somehow imply that he knew how hard everyone was working.

During my first movie in London, I had the opportunity to learn under another superlative producer, Robert Watts. Watts worked with George Lucas on the original *Star Wars* movie and spent the better part of another decade helping Lucas realize both the *Star Wars* and the *Indiana Jones* trilogies. I noticed that Watts always made the person listening to him feel comfortable, both physically and personally. He was careful to make sure the person was not in the midst of an activity where it might be hard to focus. If we were going to speak in his office, he would make sure that I was sitting down. If we were out on the animation floor, we would be in a place where it was easy for me to listen to him. Watts understood the importance of eye contact. Watts could always gauge how his message was being received because he was watching the expressions of the other person. With some people, you get the sense that they would rather be anywhere else when they are talking with you. Their eyes are shifting and darting about the room as if they are searching for an escape hatch. With Watts, you knew that you had his undivided attention. Watts also seemed to turn off all the internal dialogue in his head. For whatever amount of time he spent speaking to me, I knew that he was shutting out all of the day's other distractions.

I now understand that Watts's approach to communicating

used three essential components. 1) Make sure the person you are going to speak with is comfortable. A conversation where one or both of the parties is in an awkward position will never be as successful—especially if the topic is contentious. 2) Establish and maintain eye contact with the person. The higher up you are on the corporate food chain, the more important it is to hold eye contact. A conversation with someone several ranks below you will have a much greater impact if you keep looking at them. 3) Be present for the person not only physically, but mentally. That means not thinking about where you are going next, or what you will be having for lunch, or any other distracting thoughts that may occur. One of the reasons that Robert Watts and Frank Marshall made such a strong impression on me is that they were terrific at being committed to a conversation. I have worked with several people who were quite the opposite—people who always seemed to be looking for the exit when you stopped them to ask a question. To have cut my teeth as an associate producer working under two such excellent role models as Frank Marshall and Robert Watts is one of the lucky breaks of my career, and to this day I avoid using the words "as soon as possible" in any written communication.

WELCOME THE 'YESES' AND BANISH THE 'NOS'

I have been in hundreds of story meetings, and whenever I lead one, I like to enforce the "no 'no' rule." No one in the room is allowed to discredit another person's idea. The reason for the rule is simple—even a seemingly weak idea can sometimes lead to a fantastic solution. And if someone were to kill an idea in the early stages, then the group might never reach the terrific result. Instead of allowing people to say "no," we encourage all participants to say "yes and—." By saying "yes and—," we point the room toward an additive process instead of a subtractive one. (The "yes and—" approach is also a basic tenet of improvisational comedy.) I encourage every leader to embrace the "no 'no'/yes and—" philosophy because adopting this technique creates an environment where the group is secure to freely associate and offer any idea.

Some years after I had implemented the "no 'no'/yes and—rule," I came across a similar work method that the animator Chuck Jones used during his days directing the Warner Brothers cartoons. Chuck Jones was instrumental in helping to define the characterizations of Bugs Bunny, Daffy Duck and a host of other unforgettable cartoon icons. In his autobiography, *Chuck Amuck*, Jones referred to his meetings as "yes sessions." As Jones knew, the word "no" is an "idea killer." Group gatherings should be proactive, and the way to get the best results from them is by encouraging the exchange of ideas.

At Disney, they had a wonderful word for the process of bettering an idea that had been handed down from the days of Walt. The Disney folks called it "plussing." The founding Disney artists would always talk of how they would "plus" an idea when it was their turn to work on it. I have heard other businesses refer to this same idea as "adding value."

Here's how an idea in *Bee Movie* was "plussed." In an early draft of the script, Vanessa, the woman (Renee Zellweger), scoops up Barry the Bee (Jerry Seinfeld), and takes him to the window to let him go. This action is one of the pivotal points in the story, but it is only covered by the following couple of sentences in the original script: "There's a moment of eye contact as she carries Barry to the window. She opens it and sets him free." The script pages were then given to Jenny Lerew, who interpreted them with her beautiful story sketches. Suddenly, the written words were transformed by evocative drawings into a visual interaction between Vanessa and Barry. Inspired by Jenny's drawings, Sean McLaughlin and John Hill animated the shots of Barry and Vanessa, breathing life into the characters. During McLaughlin's animation briefing, Seinfeld came up with the idea of having Barry hang onto the magazine for a moment before Vanessa shakes him off onto the windowsill. McLaughlin executed the touch perfectly and created what is now one of the highlights of the movie. The accumulation of ideas improved upon the original script concept. The key to "plussing" is listening and making sure the environment is a positive one.

11

LEARNING TO DELEGATE

"The effective person never asks HOW will I get to do this but rather WHO will I get to do this."
—Mary Cantando, businesswoman, author, and speaker

If there is one indisputable fact I have learned, it is this: no one ever became a good manager or leader without learning how to delegate. But trying to pick up the skill during a crisis is not the optimal time, so you will need to practice this ability before the crisis hits. It is difficult to master the perfect balance in delegating. Too much dependence on delegating may cause you to become tangential to the process, while too little delegating may force you to work crazy workweeks and always be on the verge of a meltdown. Finding the right balance will depend on how much you are willing to hand off to others and how much they can handle. The more critical the deadline, the more essential it is to choose the right person for assistance.

I struggled making those crucial calls until I learned an axiom that came from an unlikely source:

> "If you want something done, ask a busy person to do it. The more you do, the more you can do."
>
> —Lucille Ball

Although most people think of Lucille Ball as the screwball redhead, Lucy was a shrewd businessperson and her Desilu Productions produced some of the biggest hits in television history including *I Love Lucy* and *Star Trek*. The moment I began applying the "busiest worker" principle to my decisions, life became easier. As much as I may dislike piling work onto the same few people's desks, the fact is, this advice works. The people who are the highest achievers somehow manage to do more.

While working on *An American Tail II*, we had a fast-approaching deadline and an inexperienced crew. The closer we got to the due date, the more the pressure was applied to the final departments in the process. Every time a front-end department (one that originates a shot in the movie, like animation or layout) on the production missed a deadline, the back-end department's (one that completes the work for the final frame, like camera or painting) quotas would rise because our release date could not be changed.

Fortunately, two excellent talents were eager to handle the load, and without the help of Matthew Teevan and Robert Crawford, I cannot imagine how we would have finished the film. Those two guys were doing epic hours, and yet no matter how much I placed on their shoulders, they managed to complete the work with excellent results.

Piling more work onto the busiest people sounds counterintuitive. Reason would suggest that a less busy person would have more time to devote to the assignment, but my experience does not support this idea. High achievers are good at allocating their time, and when they have a full slate of assignments, they know how to prioritize. A busy person is usually a self-starter and requires little supervision. In the times when I have not assigned a job to the busiest person, I have found that I needed to keep a closer eye on the worker's progress to ensure that the task was completed. Having to babysit the project defeats the purpose of delegating.

Not every project has a tight deadline, and those are the projects to be handed out to the second-tier workers so that you can develop them into becoming the "busiest workers." Knowing that superiors look for the busiest people when assigning tasks should be helpful information to anyone who has designs on moving up the ranks.

SUPPORT OF OTHERS = SUCCESS

The possessory credit is commonly taken by film directors, and it is shown with the words, "A film by _____," at the beginning of a movie. Almost every film carries the identification. All over Hollywood, agents and lawyers fiercely negotiate to gain the possessory credit for their director clients.

Some years ago, I heard Martin Ritt, the legendary director of such films as *Norma Rae, Hud,* and *The Great White Hope* speak at a screening of his film, *The Molly Maguires*, the movie he directed about coal miners. In contrast to Hollywood protocol, the director revealed that he did not take a possessory credit for his films (i.e., "A film by Martin Ritt"). He said that assuming such authorship discounted the contribution of everyone else. Ritt knew that his success depended upon the support of his crew, and he wanted to acknowledge this in the most visible way. Not surprisingly, Ritt attracted a legion of superstar actors and a loyal following of crewmembers who joined him from project to project. Making a film is such a cooperative exercise that I align myself with Martin Ritt's attitude on this topic. I think that to label a film the work of one person is often a disservice to the dozens, and sometimes hundreds, of people who contribute their talents. The person who delegates may be most responsible for the success of the picture, but that person is very wise if he respects and gives credit to the work of his colleagues.

THE CONCENTRIC CIRCLE THEORY

We all have watched a rain-drop fall into a puddle and witnessed the ripples radiate out from the point of impact. These concentric circles illus-trate one of my favorite ways in which each of us can make a greater impact on our jobs.

The key to working in concentric circles is to perform the most important part of a job and then delegate the rest. Each wheel turns a bigger wheel, which will run the entire machine.

I did not always understand the value of the concentric circle worker. Ralph Bakshi, the iconoclastic director of the '70s subversive hits *Fritz the Cat* and *Heavy Traffic*, first explained to me the importance of making a big impact.

During a conversation with Bakshi, I brought up the name of an exceptional animator who had joined Disney. I was shocked by his reply: "Yeah, he may be great, but it doesn't matter. How much does he do in a week?" I answered that he did about three feet of animation per week (there are sixteen frames in one foot of 35mm film). Bakshi did the math. "Okay, that's two seconds. So, in a year he does about a minute and a half. That's not enough to make a difference. So, even if he's a great artist, it doesn't matter. The audience will never even know he worked on the movie."

Wow! I had never thought of it that way. This artist was a great talent, but Bakshi was right. With such a small output, he would be invisible to the audience—*unless* he could make his footage one of the most important moments in the movie. This reasoning was a revelation for me. It doesn't matter how good you are if you don't do enough to make an impact. I realized then that concentric circle thinking would be essential in fashioning any kind of career trajectory.

An animated film is broken down into story segments, which we refer to as "sequences." For example, the first sequence in *The Little Mermaid* is comprised of the song "Fathoms Below," and details the legend of the mermaids. "Fathoms Below" is then followed by another sequence where we meet Ariel, the mermaid, and her undersea friends. Some films, such as *The Little Mermaid,* have about fifteen sequences, while other films, such as *Bee Movie,* have over forty sequences. Each sequence is subsequently divided into discrete shots. Some of these shots last less than a second, while others might be over a minute long. The average eighty-minute animated film is comprised of about 1,300 individual shots. While every shot in the film is important, some of the shots require special attention as defining moments.

Even though an animator will work on a film for perhaps a year and a half to two years, he/she will only be able to animate a small portion. An artist could make the decision to focus on the details of the story and animate every shot for just one sequence in the movie, but his impact as a key animator on the film would be localized to a small portion of the story. The big impact animators, like Glen Keane, know how to make their work count so the audience feels their presence in the film. Keane selects what he feels are the most essential parts of the whole story and focuses his attention on them. But how does Keane make his choices?

When Keane starts a film, the first and most important decision he will make will be in choosing which character he will focus on to animate. On *The Little Mermaid*, Keane decided to spend his time on the lead character, Ariel. He knew that Ariel provided him with two distinct challenges: sometimes she would be a mermaid and swim like a fish, and at other times, she would be a human and walk on two feet.

After choosing the character, he next decided on which particular sequences were most important to him. One of the sequences that Keane chose to animate was the section of the story where Ariel declares her wishes in the song, "Part of Your World."

By evaluating every shot in the movie and pinpointing which ones merited his personal attention, Keane influenced the handling of the character Ariel in the entire movie. Keane's impact on the movie radiated outward like a pebble that is dropped into a pond—from the specific (a shot) to the general (the entire movie).

Deciding which part of the task you will do yourself and which part you will delegate will determine your overall value to your company. If you are one of those people who is not suited to delegating and who prefers to perform all aspects of the job yourself, then you will limit your career growth.

One artist may create one hundred drawings that complete one shot out of 1,300 in the movie, while another artist may produce the one hundred drawings that will serve as the foundation for how a character behaves in an entire sequence. All work is not created equal (remember the cornerstone bricklayer?), and the perceptive worker who learns how to widen his circle of influence will stand out from his peers.

DELEGATING IS HOW YOU GROW

When you first move into a managerial position, you have a lot to learn, and your new role will demand that you acquire new skills and develop the people around you. As these new obligations will require a commitment of time, you have two options available: either you can delegate and pass off some of your old jobs to those beneath you, or you can keep all the work for yourself and expand your workweek. If you enjoy your old assignments and decide to retain all of them in addition to your new duties, your only choice is to work more hours every week. Even if you are the greatest working dynamo in the universe, eventually you will reach a saturation point where you cannot work longer hours. You will have started with a small bushel basket of assignments and will have traded it for a larger one until you are holding such an enormous basket that you are unable to move. Now you are in a situation where the only way that you can take on those new and exciting obligations is by emptying some of the bushel basket.

Congratulations—you have made the mental shift that will allow you to succeed.

The moment you gain the wisdom to pass off some of your work to make room for new duties, you have made the quantum leap to becoming a great leader. As long as a person insists on retaining control of all the work—and I have been guilty of this habit myself—he ensures his own stagnation. He cannot grow in his job. There is no room.

In the television game show, "Let's Make a Deal," the biggest winner at the end of the day has a chance to win an even greater prize. But there is a catch. In order to have the opportunity to try for the bigger riches, the contestant has to give up his current prize. This sums up the way delegating works. In order to make room for more exciting possibilities, you have to give up some of the tasks that you presently enjoy. But the good news is that the worker who delegates gets an even better prize—the time and the opportunity to make her job more interesting.

GIVE EVERYTHING AWAY YOU DO NOT PERSONALLY HAVE TO DO

Your first step in delegating is to assess your responsibilities and decide which of them you must do yourself. The key to this stage is to retain as few of your current duties as possible. Obviously, the more you keep, the less time you have available for taking on new commitments. Once you have chosen those select assignments you wish to preserve, you are free to pass off your other jobs. As soon as you hand off those functions, you will suddenly find yourself with a great deal of available time. You can use that newly minted time to take on new tasks and keep your job fresh and exciting.

But there is more to gain from delegating than just rejuvenating your job. When you pass on your old responsibilities to the employees you manage, you make their jobs more interesting as well. By delegating, you are proving yourself to be a great leader by enriching yourself and those beneath you. Once you become proficient at delegating, you will find that people will want to work with you because they will see how the others under your supervision have blossomed. When you get a reputation as a supervisor who nurtures and assists others in getting promotions, you will have the choice of the brightest prospects in your company.

Composer Hans Zimmer is an expert in delegating. Over the past decade, there have been many technological advancements in the post-production process of making a movie, and many of those changes have allowed the studios to shave off time from the post-production part of the schedule. Since music scoring is one of the last parts of a movie to fall into place, Zimmer has watched his working window shrink considerably. Instead of lowering the quality of his work, Zimmer has developed a brilliant working system where he delegates parts of the music process to the members of his team. On both of the movies on which I worked with Zimmer, I witnessed first-hand how great he was at pinpointing the talents of each musician on his team and using their skills to help him craft a terrific score. Because several generations of new film composers have graduated from his studio and transitioned into being successful composers on their own, Zimmer is never short of eager and dedicated volunteers. While at his studio one day, Zimmer played for me one of his earlier musical sketches—a catchy melody which I recognized as the "Jack Suite" from *The Pirates of the Caribbean*. Instead of insisting on performing every function himself to turn the melody into a fully orchestrated piece of music, Zimmer allowed others on his crew to attend to the technical aspects of the music scoring process. In delegating some of the tasks, Hans allowed himself to devote more of his time to his favorite part of the job—creating those memorable melodies.

DELEGATING RESPONSIBILITY IS NOT ENOUGH. YOU MUST DELEGATE SOME AUTHORITY AS WELL.

In all my years in animation, only once have I asked to be removed from a particular role. I made my request because I had great responsibility for part of an animated project but was given no authority. What I learned from my experience on the project was that it is essential to delegate some authority along with responsibility. When the authority is held back, then the delegating process is corrupted and will not lead to the best results. In my case, instead of feeling empowered, I felt reduced to a "pair of hands"—doing the drudgery work without the satisfaction of controlling my contribution. In animation, there is no greater indictment against the leadership of a project than when the artists consider themselves "a pair of hands" or "a wrist." Animation artists use those phrases when they are not being looked at as collaborators in the process, but rather just as people who can hold a pencil or a move a mouse. Whenever I hear that phrase being used among the crewmembers, I know that the project will not be garnering the most creative work from the team.

A well-regarded director of photography shared a story with me about the time he worked on a film with a first-time director. The director assembled his cast for a rehearsal, and then proceeded to describe to the lead actor exactly how he should move and emote throughout the entire scene. In essence, the director had reduced this award-winning actor to a robot who would move through the action in a pre-programmed way. The actor, being a professional, listened to the director, and then, most diplomatically, suggested, "Let's give it a run-through and see what happens."

The actors proceeded to rehearse the scene, allowing their emotions to lead them through the action. To the crew, the scene was terrific—but the director declared that he thought the results were just "Okay," and then resumed dictating his original stage instructions. Needless to say, the actors were not going to have much fun on that film, and as it turned out, the lead actor and the director were scarcely speaking to each other by the end of the film—hardly a recipe for success.

Delegation done well can have surprisingly pleasant results. With less than a year remaining to the release of *Who Framed Roger Rabbit?*, Disney was concerned that the animation might not be finished in time, and so I was asked to join Don Hahn at the London studio to support the production. My original role was to help shepherd the work through the animation department, but after spending a day checking with the animators, I realized that Patsy DeLord, the production manager, and Ian Cook, the animation coordinator, were on top of the workflow. The potential problem, however, was in the experience level of the crew. Few of them had worked on a feature film, and knowing the finale of the movie was complex, I could foresee the occurrence of a major shortfall. I went to Don Hahn and suggested that I be given the task of overseeing the ending of the movie, a scene where dozens of classically animated characters interact with not only the animated stars, but the human actors as well. With Hahn's support, I worked with Bob Zemeckis, the film's director, and Richard Williams, the award-winning animation director, to plan where all the characters would be. I was not only given the responsibility to make sure the ending worked logistically, but I was also given the authority to add in additional characters and entrusted to use whatever animation wiles I had to complete the work. To this day, my experience on *Roger Rabbit* is one of my fondest memories, and I owe my satisfaction to how well Don Hahn, Bob Zemeckis, and Richard Williams succeeded in delegating. These were highly successful professionals who put their trust in me. Bob Zemeckis and Dick Williams won Oscars during their careers, and Don Hahn is the only producer ever to be nominated for a Best Picture Oscar for an animated film. The truth is that I have found that the most talented individuals often make the best delegators, and, inversely, the people who tend to be the most precious with their duties are often those who are least secure with their abilities.

Delegating has several terrific benefits:

1 *You make your job better.* Freeing up some of your schedule allows you to attend to those tasks for which you wish you had more time.

2 *The people under you become happier and better.* Handing out new tasks to the others in your department keeps their jobs fresh and exciting.

3 *Everyone gets greater job satisfaction.* Instead of their work becoming routine, your coworkers gain the satisfaction of learning new tasks.

4 *Productivity goes up.* When people are challenged, they are more invested in their work. Workers who care about what they do are more productive.

5 *Quality goes up.* Learning a new skill is fun. And a person who is dedicated to becoming better at a trade makes an extra effort. If you have a chance to buy a product made by an enthusiastic crew, do it. You will not be disappointed.

There are two ways to run a company or department. One way is to delegate responsibility and authority, and then back up employees. Or, you can delegate the responsibility, but keep the authority for yourself—and then stand by the door as your best people leave. When implemented correctly, delegating is an essential tool for a manager or leader to create an energized team.

12

HELPING PEOPLE GROW

*The growth and development of people
is the highest calling of leadership.*
—Harvey S. Firestone

During the summer of 1988, *Who Framed Roger Rabbit?* was released to great acclaim. In today's world of computer-generated images and the seamless integration of special effects into live action movies, hand-drawn characters with shading appear almost quaint. But when this movie was released, the technique was eye-popping. The making of the film was, in itself, somewhat of a landmark event because the production marked the first time entertainment titans Walt Disney Studios and Amblin Entertainment worked together. Being exposed for the first time to Amblin's work methods made an indelible impression on me, and I decided that should the company remain in the animation business, I wanted to be a part of their future.

The biggest cultural shift that I experienced when I began

working for Amblin was a change from "I" to "we." I could tell that Amblin was a company dedicated to helping their people grow by concentrating on teamwork rather than individuality. Having the good fortune to learn in such a nurturing environment taught me a great deal, and consequently I have made a habit of deleting the word "I" from meetings and my everyday dealings with crewmembers. When working with animation talent, I make sure to be inclusive and let everyone know that *we* are creating the movie.

ALLOW OTHERS TO BE AT THEIR BEST

During my career, I have been invited to lecture at many colleges and I always enjoy the chance to meet with our future filmmakers. I want to inspire students to love the field as much as I do—to motivate them to develop their own skills for the simple pleasure of doing a job well.

I learned that my greatest value as a teacher was my ability to inspire students to seek information on their own. Most importantly, I saw that my discoveries about teaching were applicable to the workplace.

With my new focus, I tried to make my enthusiasm apparent to the crewmembers. I knew that if they could experience my passion for the material, then each of the artists would find his/her entry into making the work his/her own. Having enjoyed the rewards of working with Steven Spielberg and Jerry Seinfeld, I know first-hand how easy it is to feel motivated when you are working alongside someone who is passionate about what he/she is doing. I remember that during an editorial review of a sequence on *The Prince of Egypt*, Spielberg became excited when he saw one of the bits of action in the movie. Inspired by the footage, Spielberg described an additional shot that he thought would heighten the drama of the moment. While he was speaking, Simon Wells, one of the directors on the film, sketched out the shot on a storyboard pad and passed it to an editorial assistant, who then digitized the drawing for the editing machine. Before Spielberg had even moved off the idea, the editor cut in the new shot and it miraculously appeared on screen. The director's eyes lit up when he saw the exact shot he was describing—"Yeah, just like that!" There was no question that Spielberg's enthusiasm for the movie had spilled over to all of us—particularly to Wells, who could not wait to implement the new idea. All of us were better at our jobs whenever Spielberg was around.

There are few things in life quite as pleasurable and satisfying as watching someone blossom because of the assistance that you have given them. This is why parents love to record their children's meaningful moments. The joy of helping a beginner is what motivates a mentor. Mentors concern themselves with not only the task at hand, but also with helping their subordinates solve future problems.

CARING MATTERS

There are two different kinds of leaders and they are at opposite ends of the personality spectrum. At one end of the range is the empathetic leader who genuinely cares about the workers and views his colleagues' success as part of his own. The other kind of leader is self-absorbed and focused solely on his success. I would love to say that I have only had experience with the former category, but, unfortunately, I have known a few who I would place in the latter group. If you have worked with one of these self-interested leaders—even tangentially—then you know that you can spot these people from a mile away. As a person who has worked for a "me-first" supervisor, I know that it is hard to get excited about working for someone whose only interest is in how you can help him/her reach a higher plateau. Despite the low regard that most people have for Hollywood-types, I have found the non-empathetic supervisor to be rare. Most people in the entertainment business love what they do and are dedicated to helping others succeed.

PRAISE AND RECOGNITION COUNTS. A LOT.

Some managers and supervisors are so stingy with compliments that you would think they have to pay a royalty every time a nice word escapes their lips. I have even heard of managers at companies who believed that if they praised their crewmembers, they would be hit up for pay raises. I feel that if you want the people around you to grow and improve in their work, it is essential that you let them know when they are doing their jobs well. There is no more cost-effective way to increase productivity and morale than to show your appreciation to your crew after they've given a strong performance.

MENTORING SYSTEMATICALLY TO BUILD NEW TALENT

Captain Jack Sparrow (*Pirates of the Caribbean*), Batman (*The Dark Knight*), Superman (*Man of Steele*), Sherlock Holmes (*Sherlock Holmes, Game of Shadows*), Miss Daisy (*Driving Miss Daisy*), Raymond (*Rain Man*), Maximus (*Gladiator*), Simba (*The Lion King*), Dr. Robert Langdon (*The DaVinci Code*), and the lead heroines from *Thelma and Louise* might be an eclectic group of characters, but they have one common denominator: each has enjoyed the accompaniment of a film score by Hans Zimmer. In addition to writing some of past two decades' most memorable music for movies, Hans Zimmer has influenced many other movies, including the *Bourne* series, *Shrek, Narnia,* and *Speed* series, by serving as a mentor to the next generation of film composers.

Mentoring comes naturally to Zimmer. Early in his career, Zimmer had been mentored by Stanley Myers, an institution in the world of British film composers. When Zimmer became successful, he set up his company to create an environment where young composers could collaborate while learning their trade. Over the years, Zimmer has assisted major musical talents such as Mark Mancina, John Powell, Harry Gregson-Williams, Rupert Gregson-Williams, Henry Jackson, and Klaus Badelt. Zimmer's Remote Control Productions feels more like an experimental school of music than a professional studio. Within the walls of Zimmer's musical cocoon, talent is allowed to foster, and the results have been numerous awards and the blossoming of major new talents.

I first became aware of Zimmer's mentoring abilities when we worked together on the animated film *The Prince of Egypt*. At that time, Zimmer had two composers-to-be assisting him, John Powell and Harry Gregson-Williams. During the process of creating the score, I was impressed with how generous Zimmer was in delivering praise, always ensuring that credit was given for the contributions of his colleagues. Shortly after the music score was finished for *The Prince of Egypt,* both Powell and Gregson-Williams began their solo careers, and no one was prouder of their success than Zimmer. Zimmer surrounds himself with a broad range of talented musicians, and as the artists develop, he is careful to give them assignments that will one day lead them to securing their own commissions.

One of the benefits of the composer's reputation for shepherding talent is that he attracts the best artists. Aside from the advantage of learning from one of the world's premiere film composers, the protégés of Zimmer know that they will be groomed to break out on their own. Consequently, Zimmer not only gets the satisfaction of assisting new talent, but he also ensures that he will be surrounded with fresh ideas and enthusiastic collaborators. By being a mentor, Zimmer has created a unique working environment that not only services his company and clients, but also allows him to pass on his knowledge to the future generations.

Glen Keane, a true master of Disney animation, is another classic example of a mentor. Keane enjoys an almost unprecedented reputation in the animation world, and if you ask anyone who has worked with him, he is one of the nicest guys imaginable. Keane, like Zimmer, benefited from a mentor early in life. In Keane's case, he did not have to travel far to find a willing teacher because his father, Bil Keane, the creator of the beloved comic strip, *The Family Circus,* filled that role for him.

Few people can match Glen Keane's sheer exuberance and generosity with his knowledge. On every film, Keane makes a point of taking at least one animator under his tutelage. Over the years, he has helped many artists develop their craft, and those artists today populate many of the top animation studios. Whenever there was a need to teach the animators about animal anatomy, or the need for a how-to class on drawing a particular character, it was Keane who would volunteer. Not surprisingly, he is among the most upbeat artists in the business, and is one of the best cheerleaders for projects that I have ever seen.

GIVE PEOPLE THE TOOLS, NOT THE SOLUTION

One day when I was a youngster, I found myself struggling with a task that I knew my mother could easily accomplish. I solicited her help, but instead of assisting me, she smiled and asked, "Do you know the story about the boy and the butterfly?" When I said that I had never heard of the tale, she started her account.

"There once was a boy who came across a butterfly struggling to break out of its cocoon. The boy watched the butterfly for a few moments and, feeling sorry that the beautiful insect was having such difficulty, he tore open the cocoon. But instead of the butterfly unfurling its wings and flying away, the butterfly's wings never opened and the animal died. The boy learned later that the butterfly needed to struggle against the cocoon in order to strengthen its wings. Without fighting its way out of the cocoon, the butterfly was never able to develop the muscles it needed to fly."

Stepping in to help your colleagues solve their problems is a seductive solution. After all, by rescuing them you get to play the role of hero, and should there be a tight deadline, you get the work completed faster. The downside, however, is huge, and lingers long-term. The longer you spend bailing out your subordinates, the more you delay their becoming self-sufficient. The best approach to making sure that people do not become dependent upon you is to hold back some of your skills and make your colleagues part of the process of solving the problem.

THE EXPERIENCE LEVEL OF THE WORKER WILL DICTATE THE BEST APPROACH

Over the years, I have developed my skills in a variety of work situations. When I started in the animation industry at Filmation, I was a newbie surrounded by animation veterans—some of whom dated back to the days with Walt Disney on *Snow White and the Seven Dwarfs*. When I switched to the Disney Studios, I had five years of animation experience, but I was unaware of the techniques that the studio was using in their feature films. By the time I moved to London to help start up Amblimation's *An American Tail II: Fievel Goes West*, I was a ten-year veteran. I was no longer the wide-eyed rookie; instead, it was the film's crew that was comprised of first-timers. When I became part of the DreamWorks staff, the work environment was different still. While working on *The Prince of Egypt* and *Bee Movie*, I was surrounded with a whole crew of veteran animators. Each of my work circumstances has been different, and each has required a set of work methods tailored to the level of experience of the people around me.

WORKING WITH INEXPERIENCED PEOPLE

When you are working as a supervisor with an inexperienced crew, you may need to tell them exactly what they have to do. Although your workers may have learned how to perform their tasks at school, they will need to know the specific methods used in their new company. Sometimes the task is idiosyncratic to the place of business, and in such a case you will need to demonstrate precisely what is expected. Your ultimate goal for these inexperienced workers should be to wean them off their dependence on you as soon as possible. The faster a worker under you can handle the job alone, the quicker you will free yourself for other duties.

When we started putting together the crew for Amblimation's first movie, we had so many novice employees that I held a class to teach the group how to be assistant animators. As we found more experienced crewmembers, we were able to pair the new hires with veterans and eliminate my classes. One of the interesting byproducts of watching the artists develop was that they were able to pick up the artistic side of the job, but had greater difficulty learning how to schedule their time to meet deadlines. I have heard many times that there is a right side/left side dichotomy of the brain in people, and my history of working with creative talents seems to indicate there is truth in the concept. Artists who are excellent at both the creative side and scheduling side are valuable. The rare talents who can "switch hit" and balance their creative and planning sides are usually terrific teachers. These are the franchise employees that bring their "off kilter" way of thinking to problem solving, and who are great at helping others be their best.

Jerry Seinfeld and Steven Spielberg are both platinum standards of being able to balance their creative and organizational roles as producers. Most people think of Seinfeld primarily as a comedian and might be surprised to hear that he also excels at production. Seinfeld has always been disciplined and time conscious, and those virtues were critical for turning out high quality entertainment every week for the nine-year run of his show. During the making of *Bee Movie*, I was amazed at how proficient Seinfeld was at keeping us focused on the big problems while shepherding us toward the solutions.

WHEN YOU WORK WITH PROS, PRESENT THE PROBLEM, THEN LISTEN

Working with a group of experienced workers is completely different than dealing with beginners. You may have to tell new workers exactly what to do, but another technique is required for experienced work-ers. When working with industry veterans, the best results are achieved when you lay out the objective and then listen for the ideas. The tendency for a high-achieving leader will be to jump in with his/her thoughts, but that approach will preempt the creative process. To get the best results from your coworkers, it is best to initially remain silent and let the group discuss their ideas. As the leader of the group, you will get the chance to give your opinion, but if you impose your thoughts too early in the process, you may prejudice the working session. To use the parlance of the legal trade, when a leader tosses out ideas before the group has had a chance to speak, he/she "leads the witness." If you are someone who loves to give your opinions, and I suspect any person in a leadership role (myself included) is guilty of this offense, then you will have to learn to edit yourself. I know from my meetings with Seinfeld and Spielberg that they are terrific at "running a room," as they say in Hollywood. They have had years of experience in pulling the best ideas from people, and they have an intuitive sense of when to guide the discussion and when to listen.

13

PROBLEM SOLVING

"It is literally true that you can succeed best and quickest
by helping others to succeed."
—Napoleon Hill

When we were working on the final sequence for *The Prince of Egypt*, we found that studying the Christmas classic, *It's a Wonderful Life,* proved to be helpful in completing Moses's emotional journey. Although the lead character in *It's a Wonderful Life*, George Bailey, had a different story to tell from Moses, we knew that we wanted our audience to experience that same sense of emotional fulfillment from watching our movie. In the same way that the townspeople of Bedford Falls helped to validate George Bailey's personal sacrifices, we knew that the freed Hebrews could give Moses a sense of self-fulfillment and success.

One of the reasons that I am such a voracious moviegoer is that I often learn something new by watching movies that I can apply to my own work. Certainly, there are no more avid movie watchers than

Steven Spielberg, Martin Scorsese, or Quentin Tarantino—and these three directors are some of the most original voices in the history of cinema. Far from making their work derivative and formulaic, their breadth of film knowledge has led to their unique visions. It is not only directors that benefit from viewing the work of others. During the early days of DreamWorks, I attended story meetings with Ted Elliot and Terry Rossio, the successful writers of the *Pirates of the Caribbean* movies, and their familiarity with the films of every era was humbling. On *The Prince of Egypt*, we brought in noted writer/director Nicholas Meyer to give our film a more "classical" feel, and I felt shamed by my ignorance in comparison to his ease with recalling American and British literature. (After meeting Meyer, I had a new appreciation for the references to *A Tale of Two Cities* in *Star Trek II: The Wrath of Khan.*) Studying the work of the cinematic pioneers and classic authors has enriched these artists. We can all become more creative and be better problem solvers by examining the work of people in fields similar to our own.

DON'T IMPROVE IT TO DEATH

One of our standard steps in making an animated film is the "in-house screening." Every few weeks, the movie is patched together in whatever work-in-progress state the film is currently in, and then is shown to the top creative people.

The process that follows is not for the faint of heart because what happens is that the group gathers in a conference room and proceeds to dissect the film from every conceivable angle. Despite how painful it can be to hear suggestions and criticisms from all corners, the end result creates a consensus as to what the film's weaknesses are and how the movie can be improved. The next step in this process is that the filmmaking team revises the story, and a few weeks later, a new and improved version of the movie appears. Occasionally, however, the system encounters a hiccup.

Such an anomaly occurred during the production of *The Prince of Egypt*. The story crew had just spent several weeks reworking the movie, and as we all sat in the darkened theater at Amblin, the whole group was coming to the ugly realization that our story adjustments had noticeably weakened the film. When the lights came up, the filmmaking team asked for comments, and, boy, did we get them. After what seemed like hours of discussion, it felt as if there was not one single moment in the movie that was left unscathed. Feeling dejected, a smaller group of us reconvened in a conference room to analyze where we had gone wrong—ironically, we met in a room filled with ephemera and objects from many of Steven Spielberg's massive successes, including the original model of E.T.'s spaceship. As we sat there considering our next move, Spielberg unexpectedly entered to ask how our screening went.

Jeffrey Katzenberg, sitting near the door, looked over and told Spielberg that we had made a lot of changes to the story, and some of them had taken us backward. Spielberg nodded as if he had been there before and observed, "So, you improved it to death."

That was exactly what we had done. The changes we made to our story did not enhance the movie. In fact, some of them had reduced the dramatic impact. Altering a product, system, or approach because you have the opportunity to do it does not necessarily mean that you should make the change.

Many of us are pioneers and renegades, and much of our strength as a people comes from our drive to improve. Sometimes this drive makes us think that any change is good. Since that day on *Prince of Egypt*, I have witnessed other examples where the leadership implements a change that requires a great deal of work without improving the end result. Before embarking on a substantial change, ask yourself if what you are proposing is worth the risk. Does the effort justify what you hope to accomplish? If the answer is "yes," then by all means proceed. But if you cannot make a compelling argument as to the advantages of your proposal, then perhaps you should reconsider.

The same considerations about not overthinking your work apply to reshooting a scene in a live action movie. While I was a student living in New York, I often got to see movies being shot on the streets, and I was amazed at how much waiting around these shoots entailed. Those long pauses seemed to be absent on *The Lost World* set. Spielberg is one of those directors (Clint Eastwood is another) who has a reputation for shooting quickly and doing fewer takes. I once heard Spielberg say that he would rather have fewer takes of each camera setup in order to have more camera angles from which to choose. Having spent his adult life directing epic movies, Spielberg was experienced enough to know that dozens of takes from the same angle were not as valuable in the editing room as takes from a wide assortment of camera angles. As I watched Spielberg shoot *The Lost World*, I was surprised at how often just two takes of a shot sufficed. While most directors would have a handful of shots completed by the end of the day, Spielberg would have a vast amount. His working methods were a terrific example of using resources to get the maximum result.

BE SPECIFIC

On May 25, 1961, President John F. Kennedy went before a joint session of Congress and declared, "I believe that this nation should commit itself to achieving the goal, before this decade is out, of landing a man on the moon

and returning him safely to Earth." President Kennedy laid out a specific and understandable goal: to put a man on the moon by the end of the decade. There were no vagaries in that remark, and every NASA engineer, congressperson, and citizen of the United States knew what to aim for and how to measure their success.

Succinct mission statements can work miracles. When everyone on the team knows exactly what is expected, then they can rally around the goal. Certainly, sports teams in championship games are proof of this concept. After winning the 1987 NBA championship, Pat Riley, the coach of the Los Angeles Lakers, was asked if he thought the team could repeat. Without blinking, Riley declared, "I guarantee it." The following June, the Lakers had their next championship trophy. As Laker guard Byron Scott recalled, "Guaranteeing a championship was the best thing Pat ever did. It set the stage in our mind. Work harder, be better. That's the only way we could repeat."

Companies should focus on specific goals rather than an abstract concept of quality. A company that makes coffee might boast that they are "the best," but the company needs to be more specific. Is the company best in service? Best in quality? Best in number of outlets? Do they sell the best coffee for that price point? Are they the best compared to a brand of coffee that costs three times as much? The boast of being "the best" leads to confusion within the company instead of unifying it. Make sure your specific goals are understood by everyone. Work forces nowadays are often not only multicultural, but also multigenerational. The notion of being "the best" will be different for a twentysomething graduate coming from college than it will be for a twenty-year veteran who has a history of watching the ups and downs in the industry.

ENCOURAGE THE ALPHA TALENTS

Another aspect of leadership is how you manage people when circumstances change. As a rule, the people who are performing at the highest level before a change takes place will likely be the highest performers afterward. High achievers are good at adopting new work methods and that is why they are often the best problem solvers. Experience has shown me that good problem solvers are usually the first ones to be attracted to new techniques and technologies. If you find a good problem solver, you have struck gold because these people are the engines that can drive a company. I have known a lot of artists who gravitate toward the newest tools in the marketplace, and they tend to be the highest producers in the company both before and after they adopt the new techniques.

The "alpha talents" at a company are commonly the role models for the other workers, and when they embrace change, they encourage the entire workforce to adopt the new methods.

When your top performers achieve success by adopting changes, then others will follow, and a company can use this facet of human nature to their advantage. But if the top achievers have difficulties adjusting to the new approach, then the entire transition can be at risk. As a supervisor, it is in your best interest to devote your primary efforts to ensuring the success of your best people, because if they run into trouble, it's possible the new technique or idea has intrinsic problems. Simon Wells, the director of many films, is one of the smartest guys I know in animation. While we were discussing how certain artists seem to be good at performing just about any job you can throw their way, he said something that I have never forgotten: "People who are good at things are good at other things."

At the time of his pronouncement, Wells was speaking about his friend David Brown, a longtime animator/director that he knew from London. As we spoke, Wells detailed how Brown had jumped from one discipline of animation to another without missing a beat—and, most importantly, had excelled at each step along the way. Since hearing Wells's remark, I have noticed that his observation is correct. Whenever I have an untried problem to be solved, I always look for the best guy that I can find in a related job.

14

QUALITIES OF GREAT LEADERS

"Humility is not thinking less of yourself,
it's thinking of yourself less."
—Rick Warren, pastor

My first meeting with Jerry Seinfeld was at a roundtable with many of the studio's storyboard artists and directors. Each of us had been given the script for *Bee Movie* to read over the weekend, and we were assembled to give Seinfeld our notes. For the next two hours, we went around the room making suggestions and offering comments on the story. During the entire time—and there was a lot of discussion—Seinfeld impressed me by never being defensive or argumentative about a single idea. I could not believe how placid he was. I thought to myself, "This is one of the most successful comedians in the history of television. He doesn't have to listen to a roomful of people he's never met critique his work." Soon after the meeting, I was selected to be one of the directors of *Bee Movie*, along with Simon J. Smith. For the next three and a half years, I worked with Seinfeld on a daily basis. I learned that my experience in that first script review meeting was not an anomaly—that was how Seinfeld worked. During the making of *Bee Movie*, he never shot down an idea because it conflicted with his own. He was unbelievably open to new suggestions. I wondered, "Why doesn't he think that his solutions are the best? After all, he is at the top of his field."

As I worked with Seinfeld, I realized that his years of performing live in front of an audience had given him a unique perspective: the audience was the final arbitrator of what was funny.

I think the most successful people are invariably the best listeners and are the most open to new ideas. Before I had worked with so many talented individuals, I would have believed just the opposite. I would have expected that the most talented people already had the best ideas, so they do not need to listen to others. I've learned that what allows them to reach those heights of achievement is that they know how to collaborate with others and come away with the best solution. Seinfeld used to say that it took him a year in front of an audience to fine-tune a joke until it worked just the way he wanted. A year! That's not a guy who fiercely defends his material.

Seinfeld really listened when we played our work-in-progress versions of the movie to an audience. Because he has spent so much time performing in front of an audience, he is highly attuned to their responses. Just as a piano tuner tunes his instrument, Seinfeld listens and tweaks jokes for his audience. He is proof of the axiom that the best talent listens.

DON'T UNDERESTIMATE THE POWER OF SYMBOLIC GESTURES

Do you notice when they put flowers in a public bathroom? Or lollipops by the doctor's desk? Or mints on your hotel pillow? I'll bet that you do. And do you know why those things are put there? Because

someone understands that every contact with you is a chance to make a good impression and reinforce that he/she cares about your business. People who are achievement oriented know the importance of small details. I have worked with Jeffrey Katzenberg for over a dozen years and I can attest to the fact that he is the master of symbolic gestures.

Whether the opportunity is signing up for the dunk tank at a studio gathering, sliding down a whiz line with Jerry Seinfeld at Cannes to promote a movie, or standing in line at the company commissary, Katzenberg never misses a chance to prove that he is a member of the team. When he was at Disney, Katzenberg was known for calling every crewmember on an animated film after the opening weekend to thank them for their contribution. That courtesy may seem inconsequential until you understand that there are over two hundred credited people on a film. Even if he spends only two minutes on each phone call, he is investing over *six hours* of his time to make sure he connects with each crew person.

I remember when we were behind schedule on *Who Framed Roger Rabbit?* and Don Hahn, the animation producer, made up "We Can Do It!" buttons for the whole crew. He then went around the studio chatting to the artists while handing out the buttons, and his gesture succeeded in energizing the tired and cynical crew. Just a few months later, Hahn printed up identical buttons for everyone, except these new pins sported the revision, "We Did It!" Those buttons were inexpensive, but they made an oversized impression on the crew. When Steven Spielberg heard that the Amblimation crew was working long hours to finish *An American Tail II: Fievel Goes West*, he enlisted Robin Williams on the set of *Hook* to join him in a funny, inspirational pep video. Everyone was amused by the performance, and the artists appreciated that their work was being recognized. In each of these cases, the top talents involved made sure their staff knew that they were aware of the crew's personal sacrifices and were sympathetic to their plight. These leaders could not do the work for us, but they could show that they cared—and they did.

HUMILITY

In 1982, I found myself in a small studio off Sunset Boulevard working on a TV Christmas special based on the popular comic strip character Ziggy. As is too often the case  with animation projects, we had a lot of work to finish and were approaching the deadline. It was already October, and the program was scheduled to air in December. One evening while the crew was working late, an artist who had only been on the show for a short time popped into our area to tell us that "a guy was going out for a food run." Having caught our attention with the prospect of food, she relayed our requests to the person picking up our dinners. About forty minutes later, while we were busy working, our orders arrived and we were all shocked when we saw the "food guy."

Standing before us, holding the box with our provisions, was Tom Wilson—the creator of Ziggy! Because the woman who told us about the food run was new to the show, she had never met Tom Wilson, and to her "Tom" was just some production assistant coming in to feed us that evening. We greeted Tom warmly, and afterward agreed that it should not have been such a surprise that Tom would stop by the studio to take care of us. As he was an artist himself, he appreciated what we were creating and he made sure we felt his gratitude. Tom Wilson exemplified one of the most important traits of leadership.

With his simple act of getting us dinner, Tom Wilson cemented himself into the hearts and minds—not to mention the stomachs—of the crew for the remainder of the production. Although many people think of cartoonists as loners, Tom had experience with larger crews. He had spent time at American Greetings, the card company, where he developed the successful licenses for *The Care Bears* and *Strawberry Shortcake*. Despite his enormous success, Tom was still approachable. In addition to his understanding of the importance of service, he possessed another key aspect of leadership: the ability to wrap himself in humility. Humility is an underrated trait, yet it can be instrumental in creating a nurturing and healthy work environment. Humility allows a leader to be open with coworkers, and, most importantly, admit his mistakes. None of us are infallible, and when one of our leaders takes ownership of his errors, his actions invoke a sense of integrity. Being humble does not necessarily mean a lack of confidence, however. Humility and confidence are not mutually exclusive, and maintaining self-assurance is essential in keeping the trust of other people.

ACCEPT RESPONSIBILITY

Jeffrey Katzenberg is one of the best cheerleaders imaginable when it comes to promoting a film, but he is also one of his own severest critics when analyzing a DreamWorks movie at the box office. When a film of his underperforms, Katzenberg is the first one to be self-critical. While some Hollywood personalities defend their work and blame the movie's lack of success on marketing, publicity, or other reasons, Katzenberg is the first to take ownership for how the project might have been done better. Most importantly, he is a fierce defender of his team and his company. If there is a shortcoming, then he will accept responsibility. In addition, he is an indefatigable study of his work and is always looking for what he might have done to elevate a weaker film, as well as studying his most popular offerings with the aim of improving upon them in the future. When Katzenberg felt that one of his films did not meet his expectations at the international box office, he went on a worldwide trip to speak to each territory personally.

"THE METHOD" SUPERVISOR

Lee Strasberg's Actor's Studio popularized the technique of method acting. In the Method, one of the tools used for creating emotional veracity in an acting role is substituting an experience from the actor's life for one that the character in the play/movie is experiencing. For instance, an actor portraying aviator Charles Lindbergh would likely not have experienced the pain of having his child kidnapped and later found dead, but he might know the grief of losing a loved one. The actor can then draw upon his personal pain to portray Lindbergh's loss, substituting one emotion for another.

I've developed a technique for managing people that I call "method supervising." While not every supervisor needs to have direct experience with the creative task he/she is overseeing, I feel that the manager who deals with creative personnel must have experience with the creative process. Without a familiarity of the process, the manager may not consider the time needed to arrive at the result. Too often, soon after an artist is given an assignment, he is asked the question, "When will you be done?" How can a creative person know when he will finish if he has not had time to consider the challenges of the assignment? To help new production personnel get a better feeling for what their crew is experiencing, I think substituting one creative process for another can be invaluable. That is what I call "method supervising."

For example, say that a newly minted coordinator is assigned to oversee a team that will design a line of e-cards. While the coordinator may not have designed e-cards before, he/she may have planned and cooked an elaborate dinner. To me, these two actions involve the same process. The e-card designers will need to assess their client's needs, familiarize themselves with the market, spit-ball ideas, sketch up designs, and come up with the final product. The chef at home goes through a type of similar thinking: he/she considers his/her guest's culinary taste, reads recipes, considers the choices, plans the menu, and cooks the meal. If the e-card coordinator were to pause to imagine what it would be like to be handed the challenge of cooking a meal for twelve relatives, he/she would have a better gauge of what his/her team must go through to finish their assignment. And that is method supervising. I believe almost everyone enjoys some activity in their life that uses the creative process, whether it is woodworking, knitting, gardening, photography, or playing an instrument. If you supervise creative people, I urge you to find that corollary activity and incorporate this method into your managerial techniques.

WATCH OUT FOR SHOM, BUT WELCOME WOU

At Amblin, I noticed how they avoided using exclusive words such as "I" and "you," and replaced them with the inclusive words "we," "our," and "us." As a new employee, I felt so welcome hearing those words. They made me feel as if I were a studio insider from my first day. I learned how transformative the words *we, our,* and *us*—WOU—could be, and I have tried to remember the impact that they can have.

"Should," "have," "ought," and "must" are parenting words. Almost every phrase that we hated to hear as children started with a member of this collection. "You *should* listen to your mother." "You *have* to go to bed early." "You *ought* to eat your vegetables." And, the ever popular, "You *must* finish your homework." I suspect that each of us has a SHOM–embedded sentence that we would prefer to never hear again. Now, if you can remember how much you disliked hearing sentences that begin with *should, have, ought*, or *must* as a child, then you can begin to realize how distasteful hearing those words can be when uttered by your leader or supervisor at work. Because most of us have some negative association with these words, I encourage you to avoid them in the workplace. Nobody likes to feel as if the leadership of a company is a surrogate parent. We want to feel that our leaders are raising us up and treating us as peers, not as their children.

LEAD BY EXAMPLE

J. Paul Getty was one of the richest men in the world, and you might think that such wealth would grant him the freedom to enjoy vacations as he pleased. However, as Getty recounted in his book *How to Be Rich*, he had always longed to take an African safari, but his work obligations never afforded him the time. As he wrote, "It's paradoxical but true that the so-called captains of industry frequently have less time for indulging their personal desires than their rear-rank privates."

When I moved to England to help set up Amblimation Studios, I was stepping into a senior management role for the first time, and I knew that it would be important for me to help set the tone for the production. Fortunately for me, I had an excellent role model to study during my days at Disney—Jeffrey Katzenberg. Katzenberg got to work early—6:30 in the morning early. He was leading by example, demonstrating that he was excited to get to work. I remembered the impact that Katzenberg's early arrival had on me, and I decided to mirror that behavior in London so that when the artists got to the studio, they would see that I was the first to show up each morning.

As we got deeper into production on our first movie in London, it became necessary to ask the staff to delay their vacations, and remembering J. Paul Getty's advice from his book, I tried to lead by example by eliminating my vacation. In Europe, vacations are a big deal—up to six weeks a year and often including the whole month of August—and this personal sacrifice sent an important message to the crew. The more experience I gained in serving as a producer at the studio, the clearer it became that I had to be even stricter with myself in regard to following studio policy. Instead of my higher position affording me greater flexibility, it in fact gave me less freedom to maneuver than even our entry-level employees. When you are a leader, every employee will scrutinize your behavior. Any slight transgression that you exhibit as a leader, manager, or supervisor will be noted and passed around to every employee as office lore. And the higher you go on the ladder, the more scrutiny you will attract.

THE MORE SENIOR YOUR POSITION, THE MORE TIME YOU WILL SPEND ON PEOPLE PROBLEMS

When DreamWorks was beginning, Jeffrey Katzenberg recounted some advice that his business partner, David Geffen, had given to him. Katzenberg had big ideas for the company, and upon hearing of his ambitions, Geffen cautioned him, "Jeffrey, there's your plans, and God's plans—and your plans don't count." As I gained experience managing, I realized that many of my plans would not work out. I also discovered that my needs were less important than the needs of the production. So my take on Geffen's advice is: "When you are a leader there are your needs, and your crew's needs—and your needs don't count."

I have seen many artists move into supervisory roles, and the ones who succeed are the ones who best realize that the moment they become a leader, they need to put aside how they are feeling and focus on the feelings/needs of their team. Some talented artists failed at being supervisors because they were so used to being doted on that they were unable to sublimate their own needs in favor of their department.

Sometimes the trait that allows a person to be exceptional creatively—being closely connected to his emotions—is exactly the facet of his personality that keeps him from becoming a successful supervisor. In the same way that there is an occasional artist whose inspiration comes from such a personal place that he cannot teach his art to others, some excellent talents are unsuited to being supervisors or leaders. Conversely, I have seen some "good to very good" performers become excellent supervisors. The nature of becoming a leader means that you will transition from being responsible for your own work to becoming responsible for the work of others. This adjustment can be difficult for the individual who is used to getting accolades for her own work.

When an employee moves from within the ranks of a group to being put in charge of others, she will find that her own task proficiency is less important than how good her people skills are. Suddenly, that distant praise from our early days in grade school, "works well with others" carries added meaning.

For anyone in animation, Walt Disney is the gold standard. Robert De Roos, in his book, *The Magic Words of Walt Disney*, relates this story about Disney's leadership role:

> You know I was stumped one day when a little
> boy asked, "Do you draw Mickey Mouse?" I had
> to admit I do not draw anymore. "Then you think
> up all the jokes and ideas?" "No," I said, "I don't
> do that." Finally, he looked at me and said, "Mr.
> Disney, just what do you do?" "Well," I said,

"sometimes I think of myself as a little bee. I go from one area of the studio to another and gather pollen and sort of stimulate everybody. I guess that's the job that I do."

LAURA'S RULE

Multitasking can work well in business. However, sometimes it pays handsome dividends to give all your attention to one project.

When I was growing up in a suburb of Hartford, we had a chair in the living room that was my mother's favorite. Directly beside the chair was a floor lamp that had a small shelf attached where my mother would place the book she was reading. I noticed that my mother took a long time to read even the slimmest book.

One day while she was sitting in her chair with a hardback, I asked her why it took her so long to finish a book. She closed her book and said the words that I've cherished ever since.

"You know that I love to read. But every time one of my kids comes over to talk to me, I always stop what I'm reading. I know at that moment, they need to talk to their mother. I never know what they are going to say, but I want them to know that whatever they say is important to me. So I put the book down, *because my kids are more important than a book.*"

(If you end up putting this book away when your kids interrupt you, I forgive you.)

This is "Laura's Rule": there is no stronger way to show that you care about someone than by stopping to listen. Do not multitask on a smartphone while you are listening. Do not watch the game while you say, "What is it?" Cease all activities and focus on the person in front of you. As my mother said, "The book will always be there, but my kids will not."

As I have worked my way through the animation industry, I have tried to follow my mother's example. Unless I am expecting an important phone call, I put my phone on call forwarding when someone enters my room, and focus my attention on her. I want every person who sees me to know that she is important and I want to hear what she is saying. Instead of thinking of each interaction as an intrusion, I consider each contact with a colleague an opportunity to show how much I value her.

David Geffen is one of the true movers and shakers in Hollywood. A colleague said after a meeting with him that he made her feel like she was the only person who mattered to him at the moment. She was amazed at how comfortable and important he made her feel.

People who enjoy career longevity do so by building equity with a network of supporters. They know the value of creating relationships with others. A book, a phone, or a computer is a compelling rival, but there is no substitute for giving someone your genuine attention.

15

MOTIVATION

James Baxter is regarded within the animation community as an "animator's animator." He adores animating, and his enthusiasm is contagious. I have known Baxter since he started animating as a kid fresh out of school, doing simple shots on *Roger Rabbit*. No one is more self-motivated than Baxter. He is a perfect example of the axiom that the people who rise to the top of their field are the ones who are driven. When he came to the *Roger Rabbit* studio, he was hired along with many other newcomers, but it was not long before Baxter distinguished himself from his peers. When he was given the chance to animate the seemingly insignificant shot of a hand turning the key in the Dipmobile's ignition, he spun it into a virtuoso performance. Within moments of his shot showing up at the animation testing station, he had a crowd around the video monitor "oohing" and "ahhing" over his work. His many hours of self-disciplined work had paid off.

My experience with Baxter and so many other talented people leads me to believe that unless a person already has a seed of self-motivation within him, there is little chance that you can inspire him. The more I work with talents of varying degrees, the more I come to the following conclusion: we can only really motivate ourselves. When it comes to motivating other people, the best you can do is to create an environment where they motivate themselves.

I am not convinced that any leader, no matter how skilled, can motivate a group who lacks motivation of its own. Lou Holtz, a luminary in the field of college football, summed up my feelings by saying, "Motivation is simple. You eliminate those who are not motivated."

One of the most motivated crews of which I have been a part was on *Roger Rabbit*. When I joined the film, there were less than ten months remaining until the film's release, and there was a great deal of animation left to be produced. Now, if you cannot become motivated while working on a landmark film directed by a visionary like Robert Zemeckis, with the world-famous animation director Richard Williams, produced by Steven Spielberg and the Disney Studios, with state-of-the-art effects by George Lucas's company, then I suspect that it is time to check your pulse for signs of life. Every one of us on the crew knew that we were working on an once-in-a-lifetime opportunity, and we were excited to be part of the experience.

What Don Hahn (the associate producer) accomplished so well for the production of *Roger Rabbit* was not so much motivating us, but locating the right mix of motivated artists to make the movie. Hahn was involved in recruiting key members of the crew, and then giving them the tools to hire the rest of their departments. If you make the right choice in hiring and select self-motivated people, then your job will become easier and much more fulfilling. However, if you makc the wrong choice and hire an ill-fitting candidate, then you will regret that decision until you have to let them go. When I am directing a movie, I consider the decision of who to cast for each task vitally important. There are hundreds of small casting decisions to make on a movie, and each one will either enrich or handicap the film.

DON'T BE THE LIGHTHOUSE

We have all seen pictures of light-houses with their quaint beams shining into the dark, beckoning ships toward the shore. Such images may cvoke feelings of fancy, but to me, the lighthouse serves as a reminder of how vital finding self-motivated people can be. During my early days as a producer, one of my tasks was  to gather the best animation staff possible. In those first weeks, the core group of the studio hircd as many experienced artists as were available, but we still found we needed to develop a great deal of our own talent. As the departments were assembled, our production needs grew and we found that we were falling behind schedule. In order to boost productivity, I worked closely with our department heads.

But it soon became clear that my actions were inhibiting the department's development—by being so hands-on with the team, I was eliminating their need to bccome self-motivated. Instead of making the department stronger, I was enabling the reverse. The department's productivity went up when we worked together, but the moment I moved my attention to another area, productivity bottomed out. I had become a lighthouse beam whose impact was maintained only when I shined my light on those particular artists. My motivational methodology was impossible to sustain as I had too many departments to control at once. I was exhausting myself, and, worst of all, the results that I was achieving were at the expense of the entire production process.

Unwittingly, I had prevented the departments from developing a sense of autonomy, and hence they had grown dependent upon my attentions. I was holding them back. I realized that the only way we would succeed was for me to back off and allow each department's supervisor to take responsibility. I turned off the lighthouse and waited for the top people to take charge. Sure enough, the more motivated workers rose to the top.

"THANK YOU" IS THE CHEAPEST INCENTIVE THERE IS

Thom Enriquez is a thirty-year veteran of the animation business and has been a crewmember on a lot of successful movies during his career including *The Lion King*, *The Little Mermaid*, and *Ghostbusters*. During a conversation with Thom about how a leader can motivate his crew, the discussion gravitated toward the topic of saying "thank you." We both agreed on how valuable those simple words can be, and yet we noted how often leaders, managers, and supervisors overlook them. Thom said he once worked on a film where the director was so stingy with praise that he felt compelled to pull the director aside and tell him, "You know, it wouldn't hurt you to say 'thank you' to the artists now and then." On the other hand, Thom told me about working for Ralph Bakshi, the renegade director of the 1970s. The moment Thom mentioned Bakshi's name, his whole demeanor brightened. He explained that he loved working for Bakshi because the guy was effusive whenever he saw great artwork. When an artist collaborated with Bakshi, he knew where he stood. Thom sighed, "I've been looking to work for somebody like that ever since."

Years ago, Vic Dalchele and I were storyboarding together on the original *He-Man and the Masters of the Universe* television series. Vic was holding a copy of his storyboards for a show that he had just completed, and the stack of papers was full of red marks where revisions would be required. As he flipped through the papers, the artist shook his head and said, "You never hear a lot of 'attaboys,' do you?" Although my conversations with Vic and Thom occurred some twenty-five years apart, the theme was the same. These two accomplished men were after neither fame nor greater material wealth—they just wanted to be acknowledged for doing a good job. They wanted somebody to say "thank you." (Yes, this is a "parenting word." Our parents were right about using "please" and "thank you").

A leader ought to express gratitude. One Christmas when I was working on the film, *We're Back! A Dinosaur's Story*, I wanted to do something personal for the crew. The movie was a difficult production, and the artists had worked diligently through many disruptions. I decided to send every person on the crew (about 200 people) personalized Christmas cards complimenting them for their singular contribution. I wrote twenty cards a day for ten days. I am sure that nothing I did during my five years in London had the impact of that simple gesture—and it did not cost the production one penny. I made the cards myself and used existing envelopes. Writing all those cards produced an unexpected bonus for me; as I scribbled down a reason to thank each crewmember, I was reminded of what a terrific bunch of people we had assembled.

No act of kindness is too small to be appreciated by others. When someone delivers interoffice mail to you, say "thanks." When a coworker goes that extra mile to hit a deadline that looked unachievable, express your gratitude—make sure that the employee knows you value his/her effort. When a colleague gives up his Saturday to help out with a project, let him know you noticed. Praise and enthusiasm can be an incredible incentive. Praise has such a positive effect on us that we often recall those pleasant feelings about the compliment-giver long after we have forgotten what the praise was for. One of the aspects of producer Don Hahn that has always impressed me is how generous he is with kind words. People enjoy working with Hahn because he pays attention to their efforts, and is careful to acknowledge their contributions. Every time you have a chance to say something nice to someone, grab the opportunity. Your pleasant manner will pay dividends over time.

LEARN NAMES AND REMEMBER DETAILS

Here is another no-cost motivator that should be unnecessary to mention. As obvious as the value of learning names should be, it is surprising how often I have come across talented  people in leadership positions who claim to be "bad at remembering names," and use that as an excuse to be lazy. When a leader knows the name of each of his coworkers, he shows that he cares. I remember when Spielberg was spending the day with us in our London studio and received a call from Sir Andrew Lloyd Webber's office. The first thing he did when he answered the phone was to ask Sir Andrew's assistant how she was—and, most importantly, he used her name. As I watched this everyday interaction, I thought to myself that I could see why Spielberg is so successful. Despite all his acclaim, he has never forgotten the importance of simple courtesies.

No supervisor, manager, or leader of any magnitude should go without learning the names of the people around him. Sometimes, however, that feat can be difficult, as is the case when working with an extended crew. When I worked at Amblimation in London, I came into contact with every person in the studio, and so I knew the names of all 200 to 250 employees. When I work as a director on a film at DreamWorks, I am chagrined to say that I do not always have personal contact with everyone on the movie. Usually, I work with the department's supervisor and a few of the key people, and so learning everyone's name on the film is difficult. With an ever-changing staff of personnel and over 1,000 employees, it is almost impossible to know everyone, but I do my best. In addition to learning everyone's name, I urge any prospective or current leader to make the effort to remember salient facts about the people who work there. For instance, I always find out if an artist has children, and if so, how many. Since I work in a business where our end product reaches a great many children, I am interested in what the kids of my coworkers think of the various entertainment properties in the marketplace. With so many employees, I have the benefit of discovering the tastes of a wide age range of kids.

To some people, learning about their coworkers may seem irrelevant to management. My experience during my first years as a producer showed me the importance of the personal connection. During that time, I was working in London, and because I felt so cut off from Hollywood, I asked the Amblin people to send me their old issues of *Variety*. I was so starved for information that I used to read every issue of *Variety* from cover to cover—even the wedding and birth announcements. One day, an executive from Universal Pictures in the states came by the studio for a meeting, and as he introduced himself, I recognized his name as being listed in the recent birth announcements. I was not sure, but as I shook his hand, I asked, "You just had a baby, didn't you? How is your wife doing?" Well, I am telling you, I could have knocked that executive over with a feather. He told me that, yes, indeed he did recently have a baby and everything was going fine. My simple comment allowed me to make a personal connection with the executive, and we had a successful meeting.

Despite all the money that hinges on business and the professional protocol that surrounds it, at the end of the day, the work environment revolves around people. The more you know about the people you work with, the better you can relate to them.

PRAISE IN PUBLIC AND PUNISH IN PRIVATE

As a leader, you will be called upon to make comments about the people who report to you. How you approach giving them feedback is an important skill.

Try not to rebuke an employee in front of her peers. No matter how tough and resilient a person may appear to be, no one enjoys being criticized around others. If a supervisor admonishes a worker publicly, the supervisor risks becoming alienated from her workforce. When workers watch one of their own being scolded, each of them is secretly harboring the thought that someday a similar punitive action might happen to him/her. I have witnessed coworkers being publicly dressed down, and the reaction of the crew is always the same—nobody wants to go near that supervisor. If a reproach is necessary, the best approach is to speak to the offender privately.

As damaging as a public disapproval can be, a public show of appreciation can be extremely valuable. The sight of a peer being lauded will encourage others to work harder. I urge every leader, supervisor, or manager to be generous with appreciation. A kind word is the simplest motivational tool around. You may not be able to hand out bonuses or Thanksgiving turkeys every day, but you can offer recognition anytime.

And, on the other hand, use put-downs sparingly. Your colleagues might have enjoyed your sharp wit and sarcasm when you were a regular worker, but the moment you cross the line into company management, those once funny barbs now carry an after-effect. If your sense of humor has an edge, then you will need to be careful when you use it. Once there is an imbalance of power and you are responsible for other workers, a cutting remark will not seem benign to the target. There is a fine line between comedy and being a bully, and that razor's edge becomes more precarious when you enter management. There is nothing wrong with humor in the workplace—but the joke needs to be about a neutral target and not a colleague.

People are also motivated by a leader who remembers his/her past experiences working with them. In doing so, you demonstrate that the employee has a history of success with you. My friend Thom Enriquez mentioned how Jeffrey Katzenberg made it a point to turn to him at certain parts of meetings and say, "Do you remember when we worked on…?" Not only did the kind words make Enriquez feel better, but they also proved that Katzenberg still remembered their earlier collaborations. Positive feedback is one of the most effective motivational tools available to a supervisor and should be used freely. You don't ever want a colleague to lean over to say, "You know, it wouldn't hurt you to say 'thank you' every now and then."

16

TEAM BUILDING

*"Talent wins games, but teamwork
and intelligence wins championships."*
—Michael Jordan

When I was new to animation, my approach to storytelling was to cloister myself away and create a finished storyboard that I would later present to my superiors. Invariably, I would receive a slew of corrections—a process that was made more difficult because my artwork was almost finished at that time. As I gained experience and moved into the role of director, I realized that my working methods were ineffective, and that most successful people worked in the opposite way. Instead of holding back their work until it was finished, they sought out and encouraged feedback early in their creative processes. What I noticed was that the leaders who submitted their work at the earliest time, and in the roughest state, achieved two fantastic goals. First, they had fewer large-scale changes to make once they had completed the work, and second, their crewmembers strongly supported the work, as they were part of its creation. I learned a vital lesson: "People defend that which they help create."

When a group leader is inclusive and solicits the involvement of her crew, she instills in everyone a sense of ownership. And when the crew feels invested in an idea or project, they will work harder to make sure that the idea is realized. I have worked with directors who are inclusive in their work approaches and directors who are not interested in the ideas of others, and the best experiences and—perhaps not coincidentally—the best movies have come from the former group.

My informal litmus test for judging the chemistry of a movie crew is to see how many departmental tee shirts are created. When each department within a production creates a team shirt, I know that the crewmembers are invested in the project. I worked on *Madagascar* for a short time, and I do not recall another film set that had so many variations in crew apparel.

THE BEST TEAMS HAVE DIVERSITY

Before I moved to London to work on *Roger Rabbit*, I had only tipped my toe outside of the United States. So, when I stepped into the London studio for the first time,  I found the experience exhilarating. In Los Angeles, where I had been working, the Disney animation department was largely a monoculture of people such as myself. By contrast, the London studio exposed me to artists from different cultures with different animation techniques and styles. Because the *Roger Rabbit* studio grew from Richard Williams's commercial house, the film was using several animation methods that I had not seen before. Back in Los Angeles, almost all the studios patterned their production process after that of Disney, but Richard Williams had devised some approaches of his own, and his originality challenged what I had been taught.

The animation enclaves in the London studio were bustling with different languages, sensibilities, and styles of clothing. I believe that the originality and freshness that the audience responded to when they saw *Roger Rabbit* was due to the diverse blend of talents that had been assembled to make the film. Such diversity, however, has its own challenges, and without strong guidance and leadership, a group can end up with a confusing muddle of approaches.

When I started my job as an associate producer on *An American Tail II*, I was working in London with an international crew, yet I approached them just as I would have a Disney crew in Hollywood. The more sensitive I became to the cultural differences, the easier it was to work out acceptable solutions to the problems that arose. Since so many of the artists were used to flexible hours, we adopted a policy of allowing more latitude in when we expected them to arrive in the morning. We also protected our artists from working long shifts because we knew that we had a year and a half production schedule ahead of us and not just a few days. Gradually, I learned British idioms and became better at communicating with the staff. The bottom line was that my time in London made me more adaptable with my management approach, and consequently I became a better leader.

Jack Welch, the former CEO of General Electric, once said, "If the rate of change on the outside exceeds the rate of change on the inside, then the end is near." I agree with Welch's words, and I would further extend that truth to include the idea that if the amount of diversity outside your organization is greater than the amount of diversity inside your organization, the end is also in sight. No successful company or team in today's marketplace can afford to exclude a segment of the population. In the film industry, we aspire to create "four-quadrant movies"—those that attract all parts of our audience: the young, old, male, and female. We hope to include everyone, and so should you. A smart leader wants a team that reflects the society—because if the workers are diverse, then it is likely that the end product will appeal to the greatest number of people.

GRACE AS A WINNER

As anyone who has turned on the television between the middle of December and the end of February knows, Hollywood loves to celebrate with a series of award ceremonies. Both times after directing an animated film, I found myself at an awards banquet where I was nominated in a category along with Brad Bird, the brilliant creator of *The Incredibles* and *Ratatouille*. In both instances, I lost the awards to Bird, who is the most courteous and complimentary winner imaginable. Bird is full of such grace and generosity that when he spoke with me after the ceremony, I felt as if I had won the award. He is the perfect study for learning how a true champion takes the time to be inclusive of the entire field. I cannot imagine Brad Bird having any enemies because he is so gracious with his success and takes time to validate the people around him. (Frankly, Bird is so talented that his decision to go into live action moviemaking gives the rest of us our first hope of winning an animation award.) The lesson that can be learned from Bird's deferential action is: should you be favored with good fortune, make sure you seek out the rest of your peer group and leave them with some kind words. By being a "good winner" you win twice, and, most importantly, you are investing in future relationships.

Another gracious class act that I encountered was Charlton Heston. I have always been a fan of his work since I saw *Planet of the Apes, Ben Hur,* and *Soylent Green* when I was younger. But I knew that his defin-

ing role, and the one for which he will always be remembered, was playing Moses in Cecil B. DeMille's *The Ten Commandments.* Jeffrey Katzenberg invited Heston to the screening of *The Prince of Egypt,* DreamWorks' retelling of DeMille's story. No one on the filmmaking team wanted the added pressure of sitting alongside a Hollywood legend while watching the film, so we decided to wait in the lobby until the movie finished before hearing his comments. Of course, the main thought racing through our heads was, "How is he going to feel about us reworking 'his' character?"

As it turned out, we did not need to worry. Heston was the consummate professional, and he was effusive with his admiration for our version of the tale. Then, with the warmest smile, the movie icon addressed the issue that concerned us the most. Instead of being protective of the role of Moses, Heston was generous with his praise for Val Kilmer's interpretation. Heston said, "I've had the role for the past forty years, and it's time for a new actor to take over the part."

Successful leaders make the effort to acknowledge their peers; they understand that winning is best when it is shared with others.

WHEN BUILDING A TEAM, COUNT ON THE HIGH-ACHIEVERS, BUT DON'T FORGET THE OTHERS

Do you remember when you were in school and one of your classmates was viewed as the "teacher's pet"? The rest of the class felt resentful over the attention that was lavished on the chosen child.

That same sentiment can occur when one employee is doted on at the expense of the others. A leader may think that he is doing the right thing by focusing on the high-achiever, but by paying too much attention to one person, the leader is working against unifying the team.

Every leader needs one hundred percent of the job finished, and therefore requires the incremental gain that he will get by using every member of the team. Although it may be true that a small number of people drive the department, every person is necessary to complete the task. In sports, having a strong bench to depend upon is one of the keys to ensuring long-term success, and the same rule is true for businesses. A healthy, functioning team needs every person to contribute, and the best leaders make sure that each member of the group feels invested.

DON'T NEGLECT HIGH ACHIEVERS FOR YOUR HIGH-MAINTENANCE LOW PERFORMERS

A common lament of teachers is that they spend so much time on the disruptive students that they do not have time to help their best students. Unfortunately, the same problem occurs in the workplace. I noticed that during the early days of building  the London studio for *An American Tail II,* I spent an inordinate amount of my time with a handful of disciplinary problems. The same few contentious artists demanded my attention day after day, and I seldom had the time to visit the brilliant artists who were setting the standards for us. I was falling into the trap of allowing five or six problem workers to absorb too much of my workday.

We had one artist who made no effort to arrive on time, and his continual tardiness was handicapping his whole team. Without his contribution, the group had trouble finishing their part of the work, and consequently was forcing the studio to miss deadlines. As I had done many times before, I called him into my office with the aim of telling him that if he did not become more reliable, I would have to dismiss him. I looked at him and said, "You don't think it's necessary to be on time, do you?" He replied that no, he did not. I nodded and then asked him, "How would you feel if our accounting staff didn't think being on time was important, and your paycheck didn't come every Friday?" He looked at me with some exasperation and stated that the situations were not the same. He said that his job was a creative one, and the accounting payroll job was not. As an artist, he boasted, he could not possibly be expected to work by a clock; he needed to work when the inspiration hit him.

Suddenly, the whole situation became clear. His dilatoriness was not about his inability to wake up on time, or his failure to catch the earlier train. He was late every day because he figured that by being late he was expressing his artistic side. Thinking that I could get through to him on an artistic line of reasoning, I asked him if he thought he was among the top five artists in the studio. The artist, who was working in the animation industry for the first time, shook his head "no." I then continued my line of thought, saying, "You know, there are a lot of great artists here who have spent a long time learning their craft and they take their jobs seriously. Those artists come to work on time. If you want to be respected by them, then you have to show them your respect and be here when they are."

I'd like to say that the artist took my words to heart and changed his behavior. But what actually happened was that he was given some further written warnings and was eventually dismissed from the studio. During the course of my discussions with this particular artist, I realized that I was spending too much of my time with him to the detriment of the remainder of the hard-working crew. Sometimes a person is ready to hear a lesson, and sometimes he is not. When a worker is not receptive, the best approach is to cut your losses and refocus your attention where you will make the most gains.

Keeping the balance between focusing too much attention on the high-achievers versus neglecting them in favor of a few attention-seeking low-achievers is not easily accomplished. Moving too far in either direction is not productive for the crew, and causes one group or the other to feel abandoned. The best approach is to touch base with each and every member of a team at regular intervals while paying careful attention to the time management of your highest producing workers. Although the "alpha producers" may be the core of your company, the rank and file workers are the ones who comprise the bulk of your workforce. Therefore, these workers serve to define the personality of the company and set the tone of what it is like to work at the company.

TALENT ATTRACTS TALENT

Sid Caesar's 1950s television classic, *Your Show of Shows*, boasted a writing staff that included Mel Brooks, Larry Gelbart (M*A*S*H), Neil Simon, Carl Reiner, and Woody Allen. When Lorne Michaels started his hip comedy show, *Saturday Night Live*, the original cast included John Belushi, Dan Ackroyd, Chevy Chase, Jane Curtin, and Gilda Radner. In 1983, Francis Ford Coppola directed the small teenage drama, *The Outsiders*, which included a bevy of young actors who would go on to have amazing careers. Among the cast members were Matt Dillon, Ralph Macchio, Patrick Swayze, Rob Lowe, Emilio Estevez, Diane Lane, and Tom Cruise. The rebooting of the Mickey Mouse Club in the 1990s brought together the talents of Britney Spears, Justin Timberlake, Christina Aguilera, and Ryan Gosling. The acting roster of Ridley Scott's 2001 movie, *Black Hawk Down,* included Josh Harnett, Ewan McGregor, Eric Bana, Jeremy Piven, Tom Hardy, Orlando Bloom, and Ty Burrell. These examples illustrate the idea that top achievers gravitate toward one another. Once you have brought exceptional workers into your fold, they will serve as magnets for others.

On my first day in London on *Who Framed Roger Rabbit?,* the artists who had joined the production from Richard Williams's studio impressed me. In every department, the artists were superlative in their discipline. Over the years, Williams's studio had won many awards and, after meeting his key personnel, I could understand why. I do not believe that I have met anyone who worked harder at becoming a great animator than Williams, and the high standards he set for himself had attracted a circle of equally committed artists. A few years later, when I was still working in London, I heard that Williams was closing his studio and retiring. The first thing we did when we heard the news was to extend an invitation to the artists to join us. We figured anyone who was good enough to work with Williams was someone that we would be happy to employ.

Nothing annoys an exceptional talent more than having to work alongside a person with a "job's worth" attitude. This slang term is used by the British to describe an unmotivated person, one who might reply when asked to help, "No, mate. That's more than the job's worth." To people who are serious about their careers and have put in the time to become excellent at what they do, the casual, uncommitted worker is an affront to their sensibilities. I would be astounded to discover an "A" talent who has been working alongside a horde of lesser talents for any extended period of time. People who excel want to be around others who excel.

On the other end of the spectrum is the unfortunate truth that weaker talent tends to surround itself with less skilled people so that it does not feel threatened. When I first started in animation, I noticed that certain departments were filled with people whose sole interest was in picking up a paycheck. As you might expect, those departments were headed by equally uninspiring supervisors. Because of the extreme interrelatedness of the animation process, having a weak department in the chain compromised the final product and frustrated those artists who were working hard. I worked on one television show where the artists had become so accustomed to seeing their designs denigrated in their final form that they handed out an award to the artist who had their work most degraded.

If you believe that you are not being sufficiently challenged by your coworkers and you are not in a leadership role, then I suggest that you might want to look for another work environment. Being less than you can be is frustrating and keeps you from the success you desire.

17
SUCCESS-iPies

"Dwelling on the negative simply contributes to its power."
—Shirley MacLaine

Every discipline today is becoming increasingly competitive, and in such an emulous environment, one of the most difficult things to do is remain optimistic when facing "no" at every turn. Rejection is never easy to deal with, and I can attest to that fact with firsthand—and hard-earned—knowledge. I have a thick folder filled with rejection letters I received when I started in the animation business. I was turned down by just about every animation company in the Los Angeles area. But I loved movies, and my dream of one day working in the field fueled my drive, even after a day of fruitless phone calls and letters without promise.

The reason I could keep on writing letters and knocking on doors despite being continually declined is due to Ezra Sachs.

Ezra Sachs was my screenwriting teacher in my final year at New York University, and in a few months he influenced the way I look at films more than any other instructor has. At the time when I took Sachs's class, his script for *A Small Circle of Friends* was being filmed in the Boston area, and Sachs was a hot young writer in Hollywood. We listened as he told us about the difficulties of breaking into the movie business. He warned us that we should be prepared for a lot of rejection, and he described how virtually every script in Hollywood had been turned down by one of the studios at some point. *Star Wars*, *Rocky*…the biggest hits of the day had been refused, and yet no one lost their job for letting an enormous blockbuster go to a competitor. Essentially, he was telling us that nobody ever got fired for saying "no" in Hollywood. On the other hand, an executive could get the ax for greenlighting a movie that subsequently flopped. We learned that the business climate was far more forgiving to the person saying "no" than to the executive who said "yes." We might have all wandered out of class in a state of deep depression had it not been for Sachs's next statement. Although there is the possibility for near-limitless rejection, he said, "It only takes one person to say 'yes.'" And that "yes" can start a career and change your world.

In my case, Sachs was correct. Although I had received dozens of rejections when I arrived in Los Angeles, I only needed one affirmation from Kay Wright at Filmation to give me the boost to start me on my way. The route to your future may be littered with people who will try to stop you and dissuade you from reaching your goal, but the truth of Sachs's words rings true: it does only take one "yes" to make a difference. Several weeks into the class, Sachs invited Verna Fields to come speak to us. Fields was an executive who had risen to the top of Universal Studios' fabled "Black Tower" (the main executive building) on the success of her tour de force editing on *Jaws*. Fields's work also included some of the seminal works of the 1970s—*Paper Moon*, *What's Up Doc?*, and *American Graffitti*. She was instrumental in helping several young directors with their early work, including Peter Bogdanovich, George Lucas, and

Steven Spielberg. During Fields's visit, one of the students asked her how difficult she thought it was for a newcomer to enter the movie industry. She smiled and said, "I always say that I think it's impossible for anyone to break into show business. But then I look around and see someone who I told that advice to now working right next to me."

During those evening classes, both Ezra Sachs and Verna Fields told us the one thing that all of us wanted to hear: it was possible to make our dreams a reality. It would be difficult and trying at times, but we didn't have to win over the whole world at once. All we needed was that first "yes." Remaining resilient enough to suffer through all those "nos" to receive your first "yes" is not easy—but if you knock on those doors long enough, one will eventually open. If I managed to achieve my goal with no contacts or experience, then I see no reason why you cannot also reach your dream—provided you are willing to commit to the effort.

DON'T HEAR THE NAYSAYERS

One of my heroes is my older brother, Jim. Although he is deaf, he has never allowed his impairment to get in the way of his achievements. When he was young, he attended a school for the deaf near our home in Connecticut, but while he was there he longed to assimilate into the same schools that my other siblings and I attended. My father approached the counselors at the nearby junior high school about enrolling my brother. The school officials were wary of the idea; no deaf child had ever attended the school, and the counselors were worried my brother would not succeed. In 1968, people with special needs were separated from the general student population. The counselors, however, did not know my brother, and with the support of the teachers, Jim enrolled in the junior high school and successfully finished the requisite three years.

Next up for my brother was high school—where, once again, the counselors were guarded about how he would fare. The classes proved more difficult, but Jim was determined to graduate, and three years later, he received his diploma. During his senior year, Jim turned his sights to college and a degree in geology. The counselors were unsure whether or not my brother could flourish in a university atmosphere. But he was determined, and after successfully completing a year at a local Connecticut college, he was accepted into Kansas University. Four years later he graduated with a degree in geology. Although Jim had repeatedly been told that what he was trying to do was unlikely, my brother had achieved his goal. I have always wondered if Jim managed to prove all those people wrong and accomplish his goal because—being deaf—he never heard the naysayers.

There's a lot of negativity out there. The reason why is that it is easier to say "I can't" than to get up and do it.

SURROUND YOURSELF WITH ADVOCATES

Once you have decided upon a target, you owe it to yourself to silence the negativity around you. Negativity erodes confidence and you will need to shut out your internal doubts as well as those from others. There is a segment of society that enjoys watching others fail—just look at some of the malicious gossip shows on TV and the vitriol on Internet blogs. Unfortunately, some people cannot appreciate the success of others, and if you hope to attain your goal, you will need to avoid these kinds of individuals. Instead, surround yourself with people who support your dream and will be encouraging. In my own journey, I have found people who were sympathetic to my cause, and they have helped me immensely. From my parents to my high school and college instructors to a host of professionals, I have been enriched by the encouragement that I received every step of the way. Surround yourself with advocates and turn away from the negative chatter that you will encounter. Every goal worth reaching has a certain amount of "unreasonableness" attached to it, and this makes some people dismissive of the idea of pursuing it. Don't listen to their negativity. Almost every great breakthrough has been derided at some point in its creation. Do not let conventional wisdom build a wall between you and your target.

Not all criticism is bad. Constructive critiques by your peers and leaders can be invaluable, and it is wise to be open to listening to them. I have benefited from having my superiors point out ways that I could improve my work and myself. The first time that I produced, directed, or served as a production manager on a film, I was fortunate to be surrounded by experienced people giving me suggestions on how to improve at my job. But helpful criticism is not the same animal as destructive gibes and pessimism. Sniping is harmful because it chips away at our confidence and weakens our resolve. However, since individual success is often the result of others' contributions, I always try to keep in mind my twin credos of success:

"You can't give other people enough praise. And you cannot give other people enough credit for your success."

BE GENEROUS WITH YOUR SUCCESS

I once worked with a talented production person who decided to leave her company because a superior claimed credit for her work. Although she enjoyed working at the company and loved the top-level projects she was associated with, she knew that her career would stagnate because no one outside of her department was aware of her contributions. Part of being successful means being generous with your success, and that entails giving credit to those who have helped you. In my own life, I cannot imagine getting to my current position without the support of so many people. You will never be censured for giving others too much credit for your success.

When I was learning the ropes of producing on *An American Tail II: Fievel Goes West*, I was trained under Robert Watts. Although Robert was essential in helping me work with the Los Angeles studios, he would downplay his contributions. His most common refrain was that he was just "a part-timer" and that the excellent production staff was making the movie. Watts was gracious in crediting others. Whenever I spoke to Watts about his earlier work on the original trilogies for *Star Wars* and *Indiana Jones*, he deflected the praise from himself and said, "Oh, that was—" and supplied the name of a colleague. Watts's generosity with giving credit earned him great loyalty from his coworkers. Everyone with whom Watts worked felt secure because of his tireless support. Watts built his career longevity on the twin pillars of praising the people around him and giving others the credit for his success. Follow his example and you will find yourself closer to achieving career longevity.

THE PYRAMID EFFECT

The higher you go, the fewer people there are to give you strokes. At the bottom of the company are the workers who comprise the vast majority of the workforce. These workers have the entire leadership of the company at their disposal to give them attention for their accomplishments. Directly above the rank and file workers are their managers, and those managers have potentially several other steps of leadership above them to acknowledge their good work. But as you go up each management level, there are fewer levels of support. Finally, at the top tier in the pyramid, the chief executive is dependent on her own initiative to find motivation. There is no one else above her to reward her performance. Top-level performers must get their recognition, if there is any, from the outside. Within the company, it is their job to show appreciation for those below them.

The more successful you become, the more you will need to seek reinforcement and satisfaction from within. I have heard many supervisors complain about how they do not get the recognition that they used to receive. What they fail to understand is that getting the same amount of feedback is not possible—as they have moved up the ranks, they have eliminated entire tiers of support. The higher a person goes in a company, the fewer the people there are above him. Thus, there are less possible places from which he can receive kudos. Your success in being promoted will mean fewer opportunities for praise, and a greater need to motivate yourself.

18
LAST THOUGHTS BEFORE CLOSING TIME

"If you keep showing up every day,
at some point you'll be the one who's working."
—Richard Maltby, Jr.

Those words of advice were given to a friend of mine, David I. Stern, when he was trying to break into the footlights of Broadway. He heard them from a great source, Richard Maltby, a multi-hyphenate talent who has an extensive resume in the Broadway theater world producing (*Song and Dance*), directing (*Fosse, Ain't Misbehavin'*), and writing books and lyrics for a variety of shows (*Miss Saigon, The Pirate Queen*). The beauty of Maltby's words, in my opinion, is in their simplicity. The most important ingredients in getting what you want are repetition and persistence. Nothing is more satisfying than that moment when you break through the walls of "no," and receive your first affirmation. Although it has been many years, I will never forget that phone call from Kay Wright informing me that he had a video pencil testing job for me at Filmation.

In many ways, trying to break into a field that you love is like trying to qualify for a loan. You want the end result, but you are not sure that you want to risk the rejection. Thom Enriquez once told me that when he was seventeen, he gathered up his portfolio and drove into the San Fernando Valley to look for work in animation. He found a parking spot across the street from the studio, but became intimidated by the building—an imposing edifice that he felt was full of "masters and geniuses." Here he was just a short distance from the studio that had produced so many of his favorite cartoon shows, and he was paralyzed. "As I stood there, I started feeling smaller and smaller," he remembered. Thom wanted to cross the street, but he could not bring himself to do it. Eventually, he got back into his car and drove home without making that initial contact. Several years later, Thom was feeling more confident and returned to the studio, and this time, he submitted his work. Now, thirty years later, he is regarded as one of the best in the industry, but he still jokes about that moment when he was a young, insecure kid and was frozen in his footsteps.

I do not know what Thom's portfolio was like those many years ago, but knowing how talented he is, I suspect that if he had submitted his work, he would have at least merited an interview. We will never know the outcome of a situation if we do not try, and so we must all "cross that street" to give our dreams a chance to blossom. You have to make your own luck. Samuel Goldwyn, the Golden Age of Hollywood mogul, said it best. "The harder I work, the luckier I get." Showing up means that you have committed to your cause, and once you pledge to yourself that you will follow through with your goals, you will be on your way to success.

MAKE EVERY DAY COUNT

Jeffrey Hirota, a friend, told me a story that encapsulates my feelings about the importance of making your move without haste.

Hirota was seated next to a young woman in her mid-twenties at a banquet, and over the course of the evening, they got around to discussing future plans. The more the woman spoke, the more it became obvious that she was unhappy in her job. The woman said that she might continue in her job for another year before returning to graduate school. Hirota, who was nearly fifty at the time, looked at her and said, "You may not think a year is much right now, but when you get to be my age, you'll see how valuable every year is." Hirota then picked up the glass of water in front of him and held it up to the woman. "You see this glass of water? This is your life." He then proceeded to pour out some of the water from the glass.

"And this is the year of your life that you stay in a job you don't love while waiting to do what you love. You pour those days out, and you never get them back. Someday you'll look back and wish you didn't waste that time doing something that you didn't enjoy."

Sometime later, Hirota met up with someone who knew the young woman. He was delighted to hear that she had given her notice and moved to another state to attend graduate school.

I love it when people take charge of their lives and pursue their dreams. Whether the person wants to enroll in graduate school, move back to his home state to be closer to his family, or switch occupations, the sooner the person commits to decision, the sooner he takes his life off the "pause" switch. Do not delay your plans. Grab hold of the brass ring the first moment you can, because no one knows what changes lie ahead, and today might be your dream's last chance. As the famous American critic and commentator Alexander Woollcott once said, "There is no such thing in anyone's life as an unimportant day."

THE JOHNSON PRINCIPLE

I met Tim Johnson when I was doing storyboards on his directorial debut, *Antz*. Since our first meeting, Johnson has gone on to direct three other films for DreamWorks: the traditionally animated film *Sinbad*, and the computer-animated films *Over the Hedge* and *Home* (working title). Johnson has a theory about how people become trapped in their jobs. He likens it to the Peter Principle, the notion that a person is promoted to his level of incompetence. I call it the Johnson Principle: a person is promoted to his level of unhappiness.

Johnson noticed how often top artists would be plucked from the jobs they loved and moved into roles as department supervisors. In their new positions, the artists would no longer be animating, lighting, modeling, or doing any of the tasks that had first drawn them into the world of filmmaking, but instead they would be overseeing other artists and attending meetings. In essence, they had been elevated right out of doing something that they loved into a job that they had less passion for.

My father was an engineer at Pratt and Whitney Aircraft for many decades, and he loved the company. I recall him pulling me aside to point out a jet flying overhead, proudly detailing how the aircraft was powered by his company's engines. In the mid-1960s, he was offered a management role in the advanced planning group. Since he had four children and a wife to support, and the job would contain a bump in salary, my father accepted the position.

But I never heard him talk about work in the same way again.

Yes, he still loved Pratt and Whitney, and was a rabid fan of its products, but he never had the same joy for his work that he had when he was working directly on the engines. He loved math and engineering, and his new job demanded more of his time be spent in meetings and supervising others. I believe that my father was a victim of the work malady Tim Johnson described.

It might seem odd for a book about becoming a better leader to dissuade people from taking leadership roles. But this book is about reaching your dreams and maximizing your potential and the potential of the people around you. And you cannot reach out to people and help bring out the best in them if you are not happy. By all means, pursue your passions and reach for the stars, but be aware of those nagging reservations that you might have inside you if an opportunity arises to which you are not committed. I have seen people promoted from jobs they love into jobs that they do only for the pay increase. Be watchful of this phenomenon in your own life and, whenever possible, safeguard your personal happiness. I believe there is nothing more valuable than that glow of self-contentment that comes from a fulfilling work and personal life.

THE MILLIONAIRE'S CLUB

One of the treasures of the animation world is Danish animator Borge Ring. Ring worked with us in London on *We're Back! A Dinosaur's Story*, and I was delighted to get to know him during those many months. I would often see animators working late into the evening, and on those evenings it was not uncommon to hear the sweet chords of acoustic jazz guitar coming from Ring's section of the studio. In addition to being an Academy Award-winning filmmaker, Ring is also an accomplished musician. During one of his improvised recitals, I got him talking about his adventures playing jazz and the interesting people he had met.

Ring told me that years ago, he met Duke Ellington's band members backstage. The group got around to chatting about what they would do if they had a million dollars. Each of the members considered the possibilities of the windfall and detailed all the things that they would buy. During the discussion, one of the band members was noticeably silent. The other members prodded the quiet musician to let them know what he would do with a million dollars. The band member said, "You know why I wish I had a million dollars? Because then I could play with Duke Ellington *for free.*"

I do not think that I have ever heard a better definition of a successful life: to enjoy your life so much that even if you were instantly rich, you would not change a thing. To me, that is a goal worth striving for. I know that I have the best job in the world, and every day I look forward to coming to the studio. One of the most satisfying aspects of having a job you enjoy is being surrounded by terrific people. Animation is a richly satisfying field; it draws some of the most creative, eccentric, and wonderful people that I could ever hope to meet.

BE THAT LITTLE BIT BETTER

When I made the decision that I wanted to get into Walt Disney Studios, I enrolled in a night class at a community college. Most of the students in the class were twentysomethings who were taking the class en route to an art degree, but there was one student who was forty years older than most of us. During the breaks to allow the model to rest, I asked this older gentleman why he was taking the class. He was now retired, but he had been a studio musician for almost forty years. He had recently stopped playing professionally because of his hearing. We talked more and I discovered that the man had worked with almost every major film score composer and movie director I could name. He told me he had played violin on such memorable soundtracks as *Jaws* and *Psycho* during his extensive career.

Although he was not well known, the man was a standout figure in his field, and had such a creative drive that since he could no longer play violin as well as he once had, he decided to channel his energy into learning how to draw. I was impressed with the idea that he had achieved such career longevity, and I asked him what he thought was the secret to his success. "Well, I'll tell you," he replied. "I knew that if I wanted to last in the business that I would have to work harder than everyone else. So, when my friends went to the beach on their days off, I stayed home and practiced. That way I would be just that little bit better."

He told me those words back in 1983, and I still remember them. That retired musician did not consider himself more inspired than the other musicians—he just figured out how to work that incremental bit harder than they did. And his system succeeded. Even in his mid-sixties, he had not lost any of his drive to be the best he could be.

Twenty-five years later, I asked David I. Stern, a collaborator with Stephen Schwartz, if anyone had ever given him any great advice when he was starting out that had proven useful. Stern told me of another conversation he had with Richard Maltby when they were working together on Broadway. Maltby told Stern: "You'll know whether or not you can make it in this business based on what you do with the down time."

There it was again—using your spare time to become just a little bit better. Maybe success can be distilled to that simple of a concept. Perhaps it's what we do in our free time that allows us to be our best. Use your time wisely, and always keep your dreams in the crosshairs. I'd offer you "good luck," but I think you already know that the harder you work at this, the luckier you'll get.

acknowledgments

For more than thirty years, I have worked in a profession where it takes seven to nine minutes of screen time just to list the people who contributed to the project. So, I figured that writing a book would be different.

I figured wrong.

Yes, the process involved extended periods writing in solitude, but I never anticipated how much other people would influence the process.

Before I had the audacity to submit my manuscript to a publisher, I had the great fortune to have Alice 'Bunny' Carter spend several weeks of her summer vacation reading and editing my early draft. I have the highest respect for Bunny, and her validation of the book kept me going until the finish line.

Jeff Hirota and Wanda Chaves were conscripted "volunteers" who read the book when it was in its formative stages. Those were the days when the book was so fat, it would fill a Federal Express box—and not need bubble wrap. This is the kind of selfless act that cements people forever, and I am proud to call them my friends.

The publishing of this book has been a dream, and all the credit goes to Neil Raphel and Janis Raye. Without their keen eye and great guidance, this book would only be a shadow of what it has become. They made the leap of faith with this wide-eyed rookie, and I will forever be grateful to them.

The man who pointed me down the path to a life in animation was my high school English teacher, Jim Myers. If he hadn't suggested that I borrow Tom Brielman's Super 8mm camera, I might never have made the leap to create my first animated film. He waved the starting flag for me, and I thank him for seeing my potential.

My career has been a parade of wonderful mentors and advocates. Kay Wright was the closest thing to a guardian angel that this world holds. Don 'Chris' Christensen, Don Hahn, Bonne Radford, Steven Spielberg and Jeffrey Katzenberg not only believed in me, but they gave me every chance to succeed. Without them, these pages would be blank.

For their unwavering support, I would like to thank my mother and father. They indulged me in my crazy notion of working in film—even when it seemed like a surefire road to lifetime unemployment.

And finally, I owe so much to my wife, Cindy. In many ways, she is the co-author of this book, as she has been with me every step of my journey. If, without my mentors, the pages of this book would be blank, then it is equally true that without her, the pages of my life would be blank.